the Container
KITCHEN GARDEN

Quarto.com

First Published in USA in 2026 by Cool Springs Press, an imprint of The Quarto Group,
100 Cummings Center, Suite 265-D, Beverly, MA 01915, USA.
T (978) 282-9590 F (978) 283-2742

EEA Representation, WTS Tax d.o.o.,
Žanova ulica 3, 4000 Kranj, Slovenia.
www.wts-tax.si

Cool Springs Press titles are also available at discount for retail, wholesale, promotional, and bulk purchase. For details, contact the Special Sales Manager by email at specialsales@quarto.com or by mail at The Quarto Group, Attn: Special Sales Manager, 100 Cummings Center, Suite 265-D, Beverly, MA 01915, USA.

30 29 28 27 26 1 2 3 4 5

ISBN: 978-1-57715-755-7

Digital edition published in 2026
eISBN: 978-1-57715-756-4

Cover Image: Henrik Mikaelsen
Page Layout: Marissa Mikolaities
Translation: Tam McTurk, Citadel Translations, www.citadel.scot

Printed in Guangdong, China TT072026

the Container KITCHEN GARDEN

CLAUS DALBY

COOL SPRINGS PRESS

CONTENTS

FOREWORD

Gardens and flowers have been my great passion for over a quarter of a century. Although I've written several books about them, the idea of writing one about growing vegetables would have been unthinkable until recently.

Before I really got into gardening, we lived on an old farm near Skanderborg, Denmark. Like most city folks who move to the country, I dreamed of growing my own vegetables and herbs. I've always liked cooking, so I thought it would be great to be able to wander into the garden and pick whatever I needed. In the spirit of two old sayings— "fortune favors the bold" and "ignorance is bliss"—I assumed that growing vegetables and herbs wouldn't be that difficult. Full of enthusiasm, I tilled, cultivated, and raked a plot, then set off for the nursery, where I made straight for the seed rack. I bought seeds for almost every edible crop I could find and got to work.

I put up strings and sowed vegetable seeds in neat rows. I was so excited. Soon, the seeds began to sprout. It all looked really promising. Which is exactly what the blackbirds thought too! They wreaked havoc in the plant beds. Not long after that, pigeons attacked the peas and beans. Then, the partridges descended and feasted on the lettuce and cabbage. I made a scarecrow and covered lots of the plants with netting. It was hard work, but I still believed the amount of produce would outweigh the hassle of dealing with the pests. Thankfully, there were no killer snails back in the '80s. That might just have been the last straw.

Soon, I had my first harvest—radishes and delicious potatoes. So far, so good. But then, all of a sudden, I suffered an insect invasion. Worms infested the carrots and parsley, caterpillars stripped the cabbages, moths settled in the leeks, aphids sucked the juice out of the lettuce, and flies invaded the onions. It was a complete nightmare. By July, I had quite literally turned my back on the kitchen garden, swearing I'd never grow my own vegetables again.

Or so I thought . . .

In 2018, I published my first Danish cookbook about green food: *Slank. Plantemad fra mit grønne køkken* (*Slim: Plant Food from My Green Kitchen*). To lose weight, I had changed my diet and started eating more vegetables. As I now saw vegetables in a different light, the idea of trying to grow them again crept up on me. In the thirty years since my first failed attempt, I had also learned a lot about plants in general.

My garden is quite large, but finding a suitable spot for a proper kitchen garden proved challenging. I didn't want to get rid of the flower beds that I had perfected over many years. So, I came up with the idea of a container kitchen garden. I have always been interested in growing plants in pots and containers. In fact, I have written several books on the subject. Growing vegetables in them wasn't that much of a leap. But I didn't just want to create something edible; I also wanted it to be beautiful. Over the years, I had grown various types of kale, pole beans, and beets in pots. I grew them in colorful arrangements, focusing just on the foliage and flowers. Back then, I wasn't brave enough to harvest them. I am now. The whole idea is to use the container crops in my kitchen.

I felt fairly well prepared when I planted my first container kitchen garden in 2019. I had studied numerous books, searched the internet, and read all sorts of articles. Growing vegetables is more complex than growing flowers. It's not just a matter of dealing with insect infestations. Bolting vegetables, moldy potatoes and strawberries, kale with club root . . . those are just a few of the challenges, but they can all be addressed, as I will demonstrate in this book.

For the most part, my first year as a container kitchen gardener went well. But not everything worked out. For example, I planted kale and other vegetables too close together or in pots that were too small. The spinach and bok choy prematurely flowered almost before they were planted. The flowers looked beautiful, but it was still frustrating. Once vegetables flower, they're no use in the kitchen. I'll come back to that later.

I always learn from my mistakes, so I was better prepared in 2020. I spent the winter reading gardening books, searching the internet, and, in particular, watching videos. The English kitchen garden guru Charles Dowding, known for his "no dig" principle, was a firm favorite. I've learned a lot from his YouTube videos.

Everything was ready to go when I sowed the first tomatoes, peppers, and eggplants in March. I had no idea the world was about to grind to a halt. On March 11, I walked out of what turned out to be my last lecture for six months. Denmark had gone into lockdown. It was sad, of course, but I always try to look on the bright side. I looked forward to spending more time in the garden—and in particular, my kitchen garden. In many ways, it was a great summer, because I had time to watch the crops grow day by day.

The COVID-19 pandemic led many people to focus more on their homes and gardens. But I also think it did something to us on a human level. It was a self-indulgent time. We took a break and learned to appreciate what matters most to us, like planting a seed and watching it sprout.

Rarely have home improvement stores, plant nurseries, and garden centers been as busy as they were in the spring and summer of 2020. I hope—and believe—that this increased interest in all kinds of greenery will last.

Growing edible crops has been one of the biggest gardening trends in recent years. Fruit trees and berry bushes sell like hot cakes, and many people grow their own vegetables. Growing crops in raised beds is especially popular, as they are relatively small in size and easier to manage. Growing crops in containers is even easier.

The best part is that the popularity of kitchen gardening means that the younger generation are getting dirt under their nails. They are also becoming more aware of nature, the climate, and sustainability, which is very important. There is something intensely satisfying about growing your own crops. I highly recommend involving kids in the process. It's almost magical to watch a packet of radish seeds turn into a miniature crop in just three weeks. Potatoes are equally magical. A single potato sown in spring can turn into a small potful by midsummer.

It probably goes without saying, but growing vegetables in containers won't make you self-sufficient. That would take a lot of containers! But it's still meaningful. For me, it's not about the harvest but about enjoying the sight of the many different crops. Cabbage plants, for example, are incredibly beautiful. An added benefit of kale, Tuscan kale, and kohlrabi is that they tolerate frost, so they look gorgeous in the winter, when container gardens typically aren't known to flourish.

So, there is every reason to grow vegetables in containers—both to use and to enjoy.

Claus Dalby
Risskov, Denmark

ABOUT THIS BOOK

The main purpose of this book is to pass on what I've learned about growing vegetables in containers. I discuss the basic concepts, types of containers, soil, fertilization, and watering. I will break down the year-long process month by month. After that, I discuss the various types of crops in greater detail, including vegetables, fruiting shrubs and trees, and herbs.

My hope is that this book will appeal to a new audience—the many people who grow food in cities, in their homes, and on balconies.

I first came across the term "urban gardening" about ten years ago. Soon afterwards, I learned about urban farming. Back then, these concepts were mainly confined to big cities like New York, London, and Berlin. They have now spread much more widely.

I knew little about that whole scene before I started my own kitchen garden. But I have always been fascinated by gardens in concrete jungles and have keenly followed what has been happening in the last ten years or so. Growing in containers makes having an urban garden so much easier.

WHY CONTAINERS?

It's a good question. Plants in containers need far more water than those grown in the ground. But the benefits make up for the added work.

It's easy to explain why I threw myself into container gardening right at the very beginning of my career. Containers not only make it quick and easy to create something beautiful, but they are also highly flexible.

I always plant a single variety per container. That way you can move the plants around and/or replace them once they no longer look as good, which takes a lot more effort if you plant different varieties together.

Downsizing

People often talk about downsizing in relation to their homes, but it can also be applied to gardens, which tend to be a little smaller these days.

Some people may dream of a simpler life with fewer belongings and a garden that looks after itself, but remember—no matter how small the garden, it won't tend itself. Nor should it. It's your interaction with the garden that makes it so meaningful.

Flexibility

The great thing about containers is that you can grow plants in smaller spaces, move the containers around, and create new looks, such as by combining vegetables and flowers.

During colder periods, either earlier or later in the season, you can even move your containers into a greenhouse, if you are lucky enough to have one.

Pampering

A big advantage of containers is that you can pamper the plants and help them thrive. As you will see later in the book, containers make it easy to accommodate different plants' individual needs for soil, nutrients, and water.

Another advantage is that containers heat up quickly in the sun, so plants get "warm feet" and grow faster.

No Weeding

If you use a premixed potting soil for cultivation like I do, you won't have weeds. Weeding is pretty labor intensive in a regular garden, where unwanted invaders often overshadow your plants and steal the nutrients they need.

A Lush Mix

If you grow plants in a kitchen garden, you have to take many things into account. One is that some crops don't like being beside each other in the same soil. For example, cabbage doesn't like to grow next to pole beans, and peas shouldn't be planted next to onions. There's a science to it, but conflicting information online can cause more confusion.

When you use containers like I do, none of this matters, because each one contains just a single variety of plant. Nor will you have problems with crop rotation. Growing the same species in the same soil for years can lead to soil depletion, preventing the plants from growing properly. For example, peas need a five-year break, and cabbage shouldn't be planted in the same place for eight years.

It's also worth mentioning that I grow so many different mixtures of crops that it "confuses" pests, and they often move on instead of settling in my garden. That's only half the story, of course. No garden is immune to insect attacks. More on that later.

Kids

If you want to involve children in gardening, containers are a great place to start. They are more manageable, and kids can take responsibility for them. Radishes, potatoes, carrots, and leaf lettuce are great beginner crops because the success rate with them is so high.

THE GROWING PROCESS

SEEDS

Whether you want vegetables or flowers, you need seeds. I harvest seeds in the summer and fall, but I also purchase various new ones every year because not all crops lend themselves to seed harvesting, and because some plants are cultivars or hybrids (selectively bred varieties), so you can't be sure what saved seeds will yield. I'll return to this later.

When I buy seeds, they tend to come in large packets containing more than I need. I put the extra ones in airtight containers and store them in the fridge until the following season(s). Seeds are more likely to retain the capacity to germinate if stored at cold temperatures, but do *not* freeze them.

Capacity to Germinate

Different seeds have different germination rates. Generally, most seeds remain viable for three to four years. However, there are exceptions. For example, parsley seeds more than a year old are unlikely to germinate. At the other end of the scale, some growers have successfully reinvigorated seeds that are centuries or millennia old.

The website sciencealert.com featured an article about thirty-two seeds of a date palm, *Phoenix dactylifera,* from the desert near Jerusalem. The seeds were found in a cave in a palace built by Herod the Great (circa 73–4 BCE).

Using carbon dating, scientists determined that the seeds were about two thousand years old. They decided to see if they could get them to germinate anyway. They soaked the seeds in water and added hormones to give them an extra push. Miraculously, six of the seeds germinated and grew into tall palm trees.

Germination Test

If you're unsure whether there is any life left in your seeds or not, you can always do a germination test. I usually do this in January, when there's not much else going on in the garden.

Dampen a paper towel or cotton ball and sprinkle with a small number of seeds. Make sure to label the sample with the names of the seeds. I use plant tags and later transfer them to the seed trays. Next, put the seeds somewhere warm, and cover with plastic wrap. This stops the water from evaporating, which would otherwise happen relatively quickly because the paper towel or cotton ball can only absorb so much. After that, it's just a matter of patience. Some seeds sprout within days, while others take weeks or more. Give them a chance before you decide it's not working.

Seed Companies

Ever since I became interested in gardening over twenty-five years ago, I have been ordering seeds from England. Traditionally, the English vendors have offered a very diverse selection because they cover such a large language area. Brexit has thrown a wrench in the works. At the time of writing, it's impossible to have seeds from England delivered to Denmark.

Thankfully, all is not lost, as there are also many great Danish and Swedish seed companies I rely on. No matter where in the world you live, there are likely to be many quality seed catalogs you can source seeds from. Choosing a company that is local or regional has added benefits, as you know the varieties they sell will be successful in your climate.

Nurseries and Garden Centers

Nurseries and garden centers, like supermarkets and home improvement stores, have a pretty good selection of seeds, particularly vegetables. There is a growing interest in cultivating greenery, and vegetable seeds are making up an increasing share of seed companies' sales.

Seed Collection

Collecting your own seeds is not just a good idea financially. They also tend to sprout better because they are fresh.

Peas, beans, and corn are some of the easiest to harvest. The benefit of doing it yourself is that many come "true from seed," that is, the offspring will be identical to the mother plant from which the seeds are harvested.

If a variety name is followed by F1, beware. This indicates that it is a first-generation hybrid, which means the seeds may not have the same high qualities as the mother plant. Some tomato plants, for example, are F1 hybrids. It is not worth collecting seeds from these varieties.

First-Year Flowering Vegetables

As mentioned, it's pretty easy to harvest seeds from non-hybrid peas, beans, and corn. Nor is it too difficult to collect them from cucumbers, tomatoes, squash, bell peppers, chilies, eggplant, and lettuce. This is because these vegetables all flower and develop seeds in their first year. Plenty of other crops don't do so until the following year. We will return to these species later.

For the best seeds, select large, healthy, and visually appealing peas, beans, and corn. Leave the seeds on the plant until they start to dry, but make sure you harvest them before they fall off. Pick the pods/cobs and place them in a warm, dry, and well-ventilated area.

When the seeds/kernels are dry and firm, put them in bags and label them. I use paper bags, which I keep in an airtight box in my fridge.

For tomatoes and cucumbers, the process is slightly different. Their seeds are encased in a jelly-like substance, so I lay them on a paper towel to dry. The substance dries into a kind of glue, and the seeds stick to the paper. But that's not a problem. Before I sow the seeds, I just cut them out of the paper. The seed will still sprout even if there is paper stuck to it. I also use paper towels to dry squash, bell pepper, chili, and eggplant seeds.

It might sound a little strange that lettuces flower and produce seeds, especially if you haven't tried to grow lettuce yet. It's because of the process known as "bolting." Lettuce sown early in the season will, at some point, start to sprout and grow flowers. Soon after that, it produces seeds.

If the lettuce is sown late in the season and overwinters, it will not flower until the following year.

For the sake of completeness, I should mention that you can also harvest seeds from radishes, spinach, asparagus, fennel, and many other herbs.

Second-Year Flowering Vegetables

If they behave as expected, onions, leeks, carrots, celery, beets, and most cabbages flower the year after they are sown. Sometimes, for various reasons, they do so in the first season. The reason for this may be that they were exposed to cold temperatures, didn't get enough water, or were stressed in some other way.

From a cultivation point of view, it is always a little disappointing if these vegetables flower in the summer. It means you can't eat them. You can eat the flowers, but that's another story.

Overwintered vegetables like these always flower in spring. Instead of being annoyed that you can't eat them, you can at least appreciate the flowers, which are often very pretty. Cabbage grows the most beautiful pale-yellow flowers, which bees love!

The flowers are then replaced by seed stalks, which you have to harvest just before the seeds drop. Dry the seeds in a warm, well-ventilated room. Then place them in bags and store them in a cool, dry place.

HERITAGE VARIETIES

If you start delving into the exciting world of vegetable seeds, you'll come across terms like "heritage varieties," "old varieties," and "heirloom varieties." As the names imply, these are seeds that have survived and been passed down for many generations.

As mentioned, there is no point in taking seeds from F1 hybrids, because seedlings from those kinds of plants will not have the same qualities as the mother plant.

The first F1 seeds hit the market approximately one hundred years ago, in the United States. After many years of research and development, a new, uniform corn variety was created, with completely consistent seeds. This revolutionized commercial agriculture, because harvesting the crops was so much easier now that they had a standard size and appearance. The age of agricultural industrialization had arrived.

As cultivating seeds gained momentum, many of the old varieties fell by the wayside. These were often varieties that had been passed down from generation to generation and were frequently named after the place where they were grown, such as 'Høj Amager' (a Danish variety of kale) and 'Lollandske Rasins' (a field pea from the Danish island of Lolland), or the person who cultivated them, such as Aunt Bridget's beans.

In the old days, there was a huge diversity in seeds. Many of the varieties have now been lost. The fact that some are still around is due, in part, to the tireless work of a number of enthusiasts, collectors, and organizations who are dedicated to preserving and spreading knowledge about these botanical treasures.

THE J. E. OHLSENS ENKE COMPANY

Founded in 1804, J. E. Ohlsens Enke was one of the first Danish seed companies. It published large catalogs that are still interesting to read. It's incredible to see how large the seed selection was back then. It included many types that we now know as heirloom varieties.

After completing his horticultural training at Rosenborg Horticultural College and spending some time abroad, Jørgen Ernst Ohlsen (1814–1862) took over the family nursery and seed company in 1845. The company was located in the Østerbro neighborhood of Copenhagen, between the two streets of Østerbrogade and Nordre Frihavnsgade. This is where Ohlsen's father built the Frederiksminde nursery in 1812.

Although the company grew a significant number of seeds on rented land outside the city, in Østerbro, it grew plants in pots. Eventually, the company outgrew its premises in the city, and the land was sold. Soon afterwards, apartment blocks were built for the upper middle class, and in 1898, the 820-foot (250 m)-long street was named J. E. Ohlsens Gade (J. E. Ohlsen's Street). It is still called that today, but most people probably don't know the fascinating origins of the name.

It makes sense that Ohlsen had a street named after him. He was an enterprising man, and under his leadership, the company soon became the largest horticultural supplier in Scandinavia. He was prominent enough to warrant an entry in the Danish biographical dictionary, *Dansk Biografisk Leksikon*:

> By his uncommon energy and skill, he pushed the company to be one of the most important of its day in the entire Nordic Region. He introduced many new plants from the Netherlands, Belgium, and Germany, including trees, shrubs, perennials, and potted plants. The exhibitions he organized in his establishment in Østerbro brought the entire flower-loving public together. Even the royal family made frequent visits.

After Ohlsen died in 1862, his widow and the next three generations of descendants continued to run the company under the name J. E. Ohlsens Enke A/S (J. E. Ohlsen's Widow). I can't stand that name!

The company was acquired in 1985 by L. Dæhnfeldt A/S.

I was lucky enough to find a hardcover catalog from J. E. Ohlsens Enke online. Published to mark the company's 150th anniversary in 1954, it is a treasure trove of wonderful color illustrations and painterly descriptions of a variety of vegetable and flower seeds. I've spent a long time leafing through it. I am also fascinated by the wide range of gardening tools that we can no longer buy today—at least not here in Denmark.

J. E. OHLSENS ENKE

-Urtefrøspecialiteter
J. E. OHLSENS ENKE

PRE-CULTIVATION

I pre-cultivate plants to give them a head start. I start by sowing seeds indoors in early spring, when it's still too cold to do it outside. I am lucky to have a great greenhouse, but you can grow seedlings on a bright windowsill or under tabletop grow lights.

Some people find it fascinating to start with seeds, while others prefer to buy garden-ready plants in small trays at the nursery or garden center. This is definitely the way to go if you don't have the right conditions for sowing. The rise in the popularity of growing vegetables in recent years has led to a far greater variety of plants being available.

SOWING

The first things I sow—in February, under grow lights—are tomatoes, chilies, bell peppers, and eggplant. I plant other crops during the first half of March. Around that time, the greenhouse starts to warm up, so I no longer have to bother with grow lights.

For sowing and transplanting, I use a seed-starting mix that is porous, sterile, and low in nutrients. The latter is important because using too much fertilizer can lead to root burn in small plants. That's why it's not a good idea to sow in standard potting soil.

I put the soil in seed trays and push it down gently. It's important not to push it too firmly, as the roots need air. I water the soil and distribute the seeds evenly. In the picture, I am sowing beans. Bean seeds are quite large, so I use trays with individual cells. For smaller seeds, I use trays. I'm careful not to sow them too closely together, as they can crowd each other out. Very small seeds often need light to sprout, so they shouldn't be covered with soil. If you are unsure which ones need light, you should be able to find the answer on the seed packet or online. In general, seeds that don't require light to germinate need to be covered with a layer of seed-starting soil approximately three times their size.

To cover the seeds, I use vermiculite, a volcanic material that absorbs a significant amount of water. I keep the surface moist. Dry vermiculite is very light in color, but it grows darker as it absorbs water, almost resembling the topping on an apple crumble.

Finally, I cover the seed trays with a thin layer of plastic to retain the moisture.

Some seeds will sprout only if kept at a consistent temperature of around 68°F (20°C). At night, greenhouses get colder, so you may need to move seed trays indoors if you don't have a heat source such as a heat mat. As soon as sprouts appear, return the plants to the greenhouse.

I label the trays with the plant names and sowing dates, because it's interesting to see how long it takes for the seeds to sprout. I use plant tags that I bought online, but you can also make your own, such as from discarded window blinds. Write on them with a waterproof marker or any kind of fade-resistant pen so your writing doesn't become illegible.

You need to water the plants, but you mustn't overwater them. Too much water can lead to root rot, rendering the plant unsalvageable. Root rot occurs when the soil is too damp, which is why it's essential *not* to water from above. The plants should soak up water from below: Place the small seed trays in a bigger tray into which you have poured water. Let the plants soak for an hour or two, and then pour out the excess water from the tray.

WHEN TO SOW AND HARVEST

	January	February	March	April	May	June	July	August	September	October	November	December
CUCUMBERS					Sow		Harvest	Harvest				
EGGPLANT		Sow	Sow					Harvest	Harvest			
BASIL			Sow	Sow	Sow	Harvest	Harvest	Harvest	Harvest			
CHARD						Sow	Sow		Harvest	Harvest	Harvest	
CELERY			Sow				Harvest	Harvest				
CAULIFLOWER						Sow			Harvest	Harvest		
BROCCOLI						Sow			Harvest	Harvest		
BEANS*					Sow			Harvest				
CHILIES AND PEPPERS		Sow						Harvest	Harvest			
DILL			Sow	Sow	Sow, Harvest	Harvest	Harvest	Harvest	Harvest			
LAMB'S LETTUCE	Harvest	Harvest	Harvest					Sow				
SCALLION			Sow		Harvest							
KALE/TUSCAN KALE	Harvest	Harvest	Sow, Harvest			Sow		Harvest	Harvest	Harvest	Harvest	Harvest
CARROTS			Sow	Sow	Sow, Harvest	Sow, Harvest	Harvest	Harvest	Harvest			
FAVA BEANS			Sow		Harvest	Harvest	Harvest		Sow			
GARLIC							Harvest			Sow		
JERUSALEM ARTICHOKES	Harvest	Harvest		Sow	Sow					Harvest	Harvest	Harvest
BELGIAN ENDIVE					Sow							Harvest
POTATOES			Sow				Harvest					
FENNEL			Sow				Harvest					
KOHLRABI			Sow			Sow, Harvest			Harvest	Harvest		

*Excluding fava beans

While exact times for sowing and harvesting will depend on your climate, this is the chart I use for planting my garden here in Denmark. Gardeners in a large band across the middle of the United States (approximately in hardiness zones 5 to 8) will also find it useful, along with gardeners in similar climates around the globe.

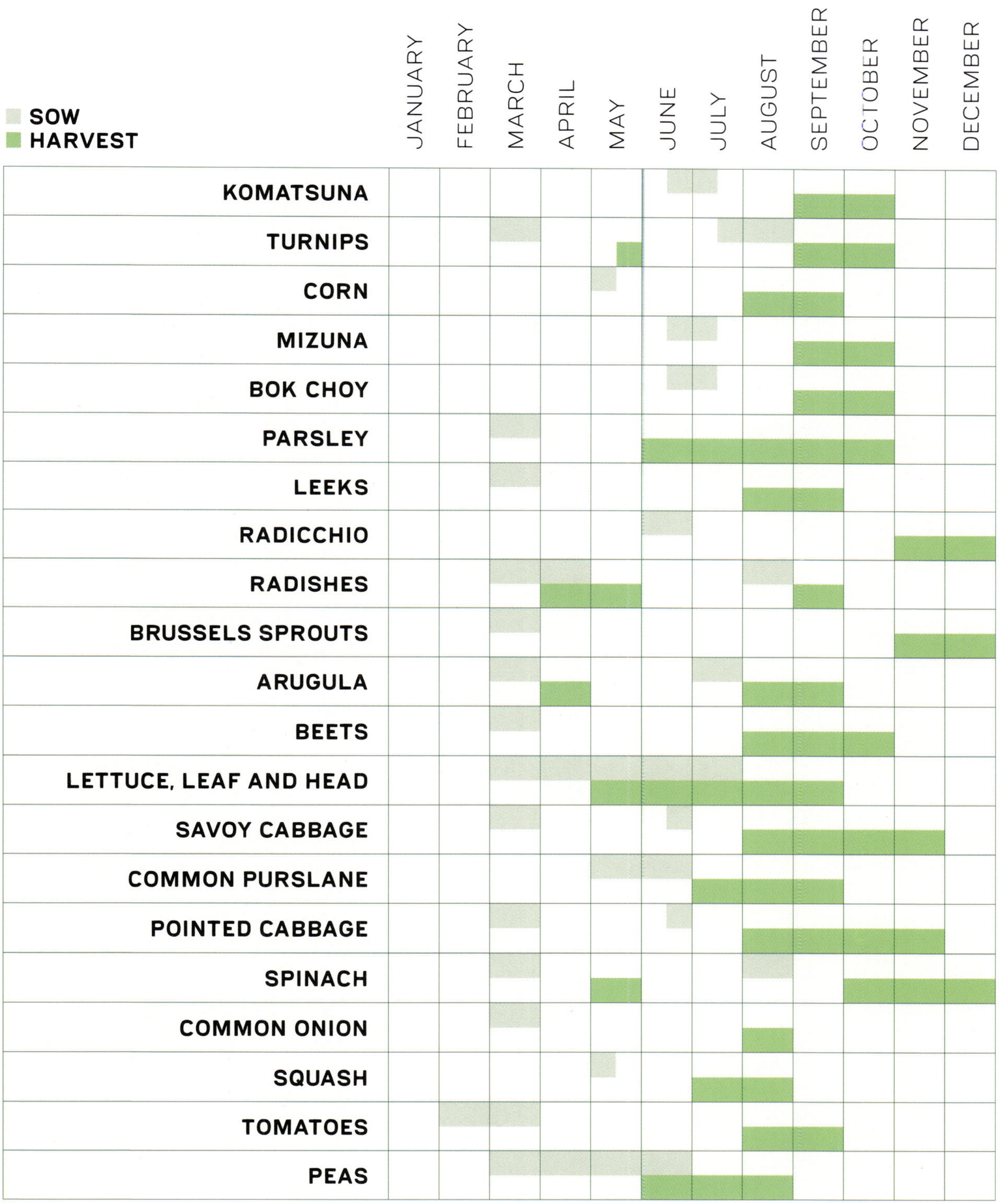

GROW LIGHTS

If you want to begin to sow seeds as early as February, you'll need grow lights. The sun sits too low in the sky at that time of year, so light is scarce. Strong and healthy plants require ample light. To break seed dormancy, you need heat. It is important to strike a careful balance between heat and light, just as nature does.

To help them grow, you have to sow some seeds, such as tomatoes and chilies, pretty early in the season. They'll grow tall and thin as they attempt to find the light they're lacking at this time of year, so to prevent this you should use grow lights.

LED grow lights are available in all kinds. LEDs are a popular light source due to their energy efficiency. They typically use about 20 to 25 percent of the energy of regular incandescent or halogen bulbs.

LEDs also have a very long lifespan. While regular incandescent or halogen bulbs last about 1,000 hours, LED bulbs can keep going for 30,000 to 50,000 hours. And because LED grow lights are only used for a relatively short period, they are virtually indestructible.

The grow lights should be switched on for fourteen to sixteen hours a day but no longer than that. Plants need sleep too!

A variety of grow lights are available on the market. Some come with a hanging bracket, heating mat, and seed trays. A heating mat is a great idea, as it warms the soil and helps create the optimal conditions for germination.

Using the right equipment helps massively. I've tried multiple types of grow lights and am a big fan of this setup. It consists of a grow light with a hanging bracket, a heating mat, and a spacious growing tray. The advantage of this system is that you can fit in a lot of plants.

TRANSPLANTING

When the seedlings are big enough to handle, they are ready to be transplanted into nutrient-enriched soil in growing trays divided into individual cells. Carefully separate the plants. The porous seed-starting mix makes this relatively easy. It's important to keep the roots as intact as possible, so lift the plants by their leaves.

Fill the growing trays with fresh potting soil. Don't compact the soil too much. Instead, tap the tray against the table and top it up with more soil. Water well. Lastly, make indentations in the soil with a dibber, pencil, or something similar.

Ease the plants into place, and gently push down the soil around the roots. The plants won't grow for the first few days after you transplant them but will soon settle in. You'll be surprised how quickly they grow!

When the roots start to protrude from the holes in the bottom of the tray, repot them either directly into larger containers or into gradually bigger ones.

GREENHOUSES

The greenhouse was a brilliant invention. I'm lucky to have several, and I don't know what I'd do without them. They're the backbone of my garden. I use them to pre-cultivate vegetables for my container kitchen garden as well as flowers for my beds.

Of course, I'm aware not everyone has a greenhouse or has room for one. But I'd like to make a case for smaller greenhouses. One of my favorites is shown in this photo. It's basically a 4 x 4-foot (120 x 120 cm) raised bed with a canopy, available in two different heights, 1 or 1½ feet tall (30 or 50 cm). They hold 95 and 172 gallons of soil (360 and 650 liters), respectively.

The canopy is 3⅓ feet tall (100 cm), constructed out of aluminum poles, and fitted with a heavy-duty plastic cover secured to the poles with hook-and-loop fasteners. It also includes insect netting.

The benefit of this type of greenhouse is that you can remove the plastic cover on hot days and replace it when the temperature drops. To make the most of the space, you can also mount shelves or plant trays towards the top.

Other mini-greenhouses come mounted on pallet frames. They work a bit like cold frames. I also have a small greenhouse as shown in the picture on the next page. It is approximately 2⅔ x 4 feet (80 x 120 cm), the dimensions of a standard European pallet. The frame is made of aluminum, with glass sides, and the windows open. When setting up this type of greenhouse, always turn the pallet frame upside down so the corner brackets keep the greenhouse in place.

REPOTTING

To encourage plants to grow as quickly as possible, gardeners repot plants into incrementally larger pots, increasing the diameter a couple of centimeters each time.

You might wonder why you can't simply place a smaller plant in a large pot from the start and achieve the same result. The reason is that the roots will get lost, quite literally, if there's too much soil. In my opinion, plants only really feel at home when their roots touch the sides and bottom of the pot.

Each time you repot a plant, top the new pot up with fresh soil, but remember not to compress it too much.

When I talk about "pots," I mean small plastic ones. By "containers," I mean larger receptacles in which the established plants grow. Usually, they are larger clay pots, but as we will discuss in the next section, various other types are available.

PLANTING

TYPES OF CONTAINERS

I usually use clay pots, but I also have boxes, buckets, and tubs in my garden. I like the variation in shapes and materials. I want my garden to look casual but planned.

A common denominator for all of the containers is that they have drainage holes in the bottom. If water pools, it can cut off the supply of oxygen to the plants' roots, and they can drown.

Containers made for outdoor use always have holes in the bottom. Ones like clay pots come with saucers. However, I don't use saucers, as they overflow when I water my plants.

I often get asked how to stop ants from getting into containers. This is a common problem, so here's a tip from a friend with an ant-riddled garden. Before filling the container with soil, line the bottom with a disposable dishcloth. This covers the holes, meaning the ants can't get in, but the water can get out. Now, isn't that smart?

Another frequently asked question is about drainage. Some people cover the bottom of the container with pebbles or shards of broken pottery before adding soil. The idea is to avoid clogging the drainage hole(s), but if they're large enough, that shouldn't be a problem. I just make sure they are. If the holes are too small, I make them bigger using a drill with a masonry bit. That means I don't need to take any additional drainage measures.

CLAY POTS

I mostly choose clay pots, but I also like the raw look of concrete. The beauty of these materials is that that over time, they develop a patina, which adds character. Many people seem to appreciate the aged look, as the patinated containers in my social media posts often prompt questions about what I do to achieve that effect. My answer is nothing! It happens all on its own.

However, the website of the Danish Garden Society offers some tips that might be worth a try:

- Find a couple of handfuls of moss, perhaps on the roof of your house or shed.
- Rinse the moss to get rid of any small rocks or dirt.
- Chop the moss with a parsley chopper or in an old blender.
- Mix buttermilk with the chopped moss—about the same amount as mayonnaise in a potato salad.
- Spread the buttermilk-moss mixture on your pots. The best time to do this is during the fall or spring, when conditions are not too dry.
- Regularly moisten the moss with a spray until it is fully affixed to the pot.

I am always on the lookout for new containers. One requirement is that they are unglazed and modest in shape and size. A glaze is practical because it keeps the moisture in the soil from evaporating as quickly, but I still prefer unglazed materials, as the containers blend in well with the plants and don't generate too much visual "noise."

CRATES AND BOXES

Rectangular crates and boxes work very well in the garden. The straight lines provide contrast to the roundness of the clay pots.

I´m particularly fond of metal ones, and I´m lucky enough to own an extensive collection of metal lobster crates—at least that´s what they were sold to me as about ten years ago. I´m told they were once used for storing lobsters, but they´re now quite popular with gardeners here in Denmark. The raw, rustic, industrial look is perfect for kitchen herbs.

From a gardener´s perspective, the large holes on the sides of these crates aren´t great, because soil spills out. But a bit of roofing felt lining the boxes will stop that.

You can also use various other types of crates and boxes, such as old wooden apple crates. While they look beautiful, they aren´t very durable.

Balcony planters are another option. More and more people have balconies these days, and they are a great place to grow edible crops like herbs. I don´t have a balcony myself, but I do have planters under my windows, in which I grow a mix of edible and flowering herbs. It´s important to use every square inch of space, especially when you don´t have many of them to play with.

BUCKETS AND TUBS

In flea markets or online, you might be lucky enough to find old zinc washtubs that make ideal planters. We didn't have a bathroom when I was a kid, and I remember being scrubbed down in one of those in the basement! I don't remember if all of us kids shared the same water, but many families did.

These tubs weren't intended to be baths. They were used for washing clothes, and, like washboards, they were indispensable household items before the advent of the washing machine.

I have picked mine up from all sorts of places. Some are probably from Eastern Europe, because demand has stripped the Danish market bare. In the old days, people would have just thrown the tubs out once they'd served their purpose, but that's no longer the case. Nowadays, people know what they're worth.

I also use old barrels as planters, including used wine barrels that have been cut in half and painted black. At one point, I was also lucky to find some not very tall ones that are extremely pretty (see page 102).

LIGHTWEIGHT POTS AND GROW BAGS

Lightweight pots and other containers have become popular in recent years. They're not too heavy and so easy to handle, which is great, especially on a balcony. It's also an advantage in a bigger garden. I have no doubt that we will see more of them in the future.

As demand has taken off, supply has matched it. Many of the pots are lookalikes, lightweight fiberglass pots made to resemble other materials, like clay or metal.

The first lightweight pots on the market looked a bit artificial, so I wasn't a big fan. Luckily, techniques have improved, and some of the new fiberglass pots have a nice finish and don't look half bad.

Grow bags—a relatively new product—are worth a mention too. Made of fabric or plastic, they weigh little and don't cost much.

SOIL

A successful container garden needs good soil. Some people buy bags of cheap soil, slice them open, and pour it into their containers. I would recommend not doing that. Quality and price go hand in hand. Those cheap bags of soil on sale at nurseries and garden centers are often of poor quality. Never skimp on your soil. Quality is worth paying for. Pamper your plants, and you'll get more out of them.

My Own Soil

It will come as little surprise to readers in Denmark that I use my own soil, Claus Dalby Pot Soil, which I developed in collaboration with Pindstrup, a Danish producer of garden substrates, and Bilka, a Danish store chain. It is a top-notch mixture of cow-manure-based compost, clay granules, and, most importantly, a slow-release fertilizer with enough nutrients to last an entire season. Whatever you grow, it will thrive on this mixture. The good thing is that the fertilizer works well not only for vegetables but also for every other kind of crop. Even cabbage, which needs a lot of fertilizer, won't need any extra nutrients.

In my first season as a kitchen gardener, I tested various types of soil, including organic types and organic fertilizers, and they worked well.

Mixing Soil at Home

For readers in the United States and elsewhere, there are many commercial brands of potting soil available, but remember that you get what you pay for. It's also possible to mix your own soil blends at home. Nowadays, we try to minimize the use of sphagnum peat, a slow-growing moss species. It's a limited natural resource and takes a very long time to recover.

I have many gardening friends who have never used sphagnum in their garden. My friend Jens Juhl makes his own potting soil from two parts garden soil, one part compost, and one part sand, which he sifts. Keep in mind that the soil varies from garden to garden, so take the mixing ratio with a grain of salt.

Recycling

Every now and then I am asked whether I recycle the soil in my pots. Some of it, yes. I reuse the soil for lettuce, which doesn't need much nutrition. The same goes for a number of summer flowers, such as nasturtiums and marigolds, all of which thrive in low-nutrient soil.

When it comes to recycling soil, it is crucial to think about one thing: crop rotation. That's why I often reuse potting soil by adding it to my beds, which is a form of recycling.

CARE

WATERING

Some of the most common queries about growing plants in containers concern watering. In summer, you need to water your plants often, but it's difficult to keep on top of that during the vacation season.

One solution is an automatic system that connects your hoses to a tap and more or less takes care of itself. I don't have anything like that because the hoses spoil the look I'm after in my garden. Also, I don't mind watering. In fact, I enjoy walking around and "talking" to my plants while I do it. I'm also lucky enough to have someone who helps if I'm away for a while. But when I'm at home, I usually do it myself.

The water pressure is good where I live, which helps when you have a lot of plants. The right equipment also makes a big difference. Having tried many options over the years, look for durable metal equipment whenever possible to meet your needs.

I use a soft rain nozzle, which is a rod with a showerhead-like attachment.

FERTILIZERS

Obviously, plants need nutrients. Like humans, vitamins are also good for them.

Different crops need different amounts of nutrients, though. For example, lettuce hardly needs any, while every type of cabbage needs a lot.

As mentioned, I use a soil blend that contains a slow-release fertilizer, and I don't use different fertilizers on different crops. The pictures in this book serve as testimony that my plants get all the nutrients they need.

NATURAL FERTILIZERS

Organic kitchen gardens using natural fertilizers are popular. The organic material can be manure, compost, an animal processing byproduct, or a mined mineral. Organic fertilizers are great, not just from an environmental perspective but also because they are absorbed slowly, which reduces the risk of overfertilization, which can happen with artificial fertilizers. That's not to say that natural fertilizers are entirely harmless. You have to be careful when using manure, especially in spring. Avoid direct contact with the plants and their roots. It is also best to fully compost the manure first.

Before using the manure, leave it alone for a few months. Otherwise, it might be too powerful. You can always test its strength by sowing some cress seeds (or other fast-sprouting seeds) in it. If they die or fail to sprout, wait a little longer.

I found an excellent summary on the Danish Garden Society's website, which I have paraphrased here:

When you use artificial fertilizer, you know exactly how many nutrients it contains, which makes it easy to calculate how much each plant needs.

When you use an organic fertilizer, like compost or manure, it's not that easy. The nutrient content can vary greatly depending on the composition of the compost, how much straw is in the manure, and how old the manure is.

Organic fertilizers not only provide nutrients, but also improve the soil. Microorganisms break down the organic material in them, which makes the structure of the soil lighter and more porous. This leaves more room for roots to develop, which means the plants will grow better.

Manure

How much manure should you use? That's a tough one, because the nutrient content varies wildly, depending on factors like how much the manure has decomposed or how much straw it contains.

For plants that need a lot of nutrients, you usually need to supplement with another kind of fertilizer that contains more nitrogen. How much you add depends on which animal produced the manure.

Horse Manure

Fresh horse manure contains approximately 0.5 to 0.7% nitrogen, 0.6 to 3.0% phosphorus, and 0.6 to 4.0% potassium. It's essential to keep in mind that the most readily available nutrients are released in the first few weeks. After that, the organic matter slowly decomposes over several years.

Chicken Manure

Chicken manure is a little stronger. It contains about three times as much nitrogen as horse manure and more nutrients that plants can readily absorb.

If you use too much, you risk burning your plant. The best option is to add chicken manure to your compost so it breaks down before you use it.

Rabbit Manure

Rabbit manure contains even more nitrogen than chicken manure, which means you need to be even more careful not to burn your plants.

Compost

Composting food scraps and garden waste is a great way to produce environmentally friendly fertilizer.

The quantities of nitrogen and other nutrients in your compost largely depend on the ratio of "green" and "brown" plant waste. Green plant materials like vegetable peelings, untreated grass clippings, and coffee grounds contain the most nitrogen. Brown—or dry—garden waste, such as branches, stems, twigs, and weathered leaves, contains less.

Your compost is ready for use when it is dark in color, is loose in texture, and has an earthy smell. But don't leave it too long, as the microorganisms in the soil need to feed on organic material that has not yet broken down. This helps nutrients release over time as the plant needs them.

Mass-Produced Organic Fertilizer

Mass-produced organic fertilizers are another option. These are often dry, odorless pellets with a higher nutrient content than fresh manure. The exact nutrient ratio is usually printed on the packaging. Some contain added minerals for a more balanced nutrient composition.

Mass-produced organic fertilizers have two distinct advantages: they don't burn plants, and it's easy to calculate the dosage.

Liquid Fertilizer

You can use plant extracts to make your own liquid fertilizer. Young nettles are especially suitable, but you can also use comfrey, horsetail, or a mixture of weeds.

There are many different recipes out there, and they are all based on the same principle: Put approximately 2 pounds (1 kilogram) of herbs in a large bucket or barrel with just over 2.6 gallons (10 liters) of water, and leave it until the water turns brown. Stir every couple of days.

Five days is long enough to extract most of the nutrients and short enough to stop the water from smelling putrid. When watering, mix one part concentrate with ten parts water.

You can also buy organic liquid fertilizer made from various ingredients, including kelp and seaweed.

Artificial Fertilizer

When we talk about artificial fertilizer, we often mention NPK, which stands for nitrogen (N), phosphorus (P), and potassium (K). Fertilizers frequently have other added nutrients, too, in the form of mineral salts and micronutrients.

NPK fertilizers are often granulated and sprinkled over beds. They then dissolve in the rain and are absorbed by the soil. I don't recommend using these types of fertilizer in containers, because it's difficult to get the dose right. Instead, use a liquid fertilizer, such as a greenhouse fertilizer.

Ready-mixed concentrate is quite expensive. Powdered fertilizer is cheaper. You mix it with water to form a concentrate, which you dilute when watering the plants.

Another option is to mix slow-release fertilizer into your soil. It is available in pelleted form, which makes it easy to dose.

Cabbages are hungry plants. Feed them well and they'll grow well, especially if you plant them in large containers with good soil. This Savoy cabbage has really taken off.

BOLTING

The term *bolting* is a bit tricky to explain and only really makes sense once you've seen onions or lettuce sprout, flower, and set seed. While the flowers look beautiful, kitchen gardeners are usually not too thrilled about their arrival—especially when it happens prematurely, as it means the crops are no use for cooking.

I say "prematurely" because vegetables sometimes bloom before we have a chance to pick them. Broccoli and cauliflower, for example, might develop flowers before the heads are fully developed, especially early in the season. It's more likely to happen if you sow early. The same is true of spinach, bok choy, and some Asian greens.

Bolting can happen for many reasons. One is a burst of colder weather. When the temperature rises again, the plants assume they've survived the winter and start to bloom. Another reason is dry soil. Plants will do everything they can to survive, so they begin to bloom. The third reason might be the plants have been cultivated at the wrong time. For example, growing a crop that prefers cooler weather during the heat of summer can cause it to bolt. Later in this book, I will go into more detail on the optimal conditions for different crops.

Bottom: Vegetables that overwinter will flower the following spring. Both you and the bees can enjoy the flowers as they are, but you can also eat them.

Opposite: Don't despair if your leeks sprout and flower. They look great, and you can collect the seeds later in the season.

TO USE AND ENJOY

AESTHETICS

For as long as I can remember, I've loved arranging, staging, and decorating. Aesthetics mean a lot to me, and I have taken that passion into the garden. For me, it isn't enough for a plant to just be pretty on its own. I want all of my plants to bring out the best in each other, so I group them and combine them to create a whole picture.

The main point of a kitchen garden is to put food on the table, but more and more people are recognizing the beauty of vegetables and now grow them alongside their flowers. This isn't a new phenomenon, and we even have a name for this type of garden: *potager*.

POTAGER GARDENS

Originating from France, *potager* basically means a place where herbs and vegetables are grown. The English embraced the word many moons ago and coined the term "potager garden" to describe gardens where flowers and vegetables form a symbiotic whole. Nowadays, people tend to grow flowers in them for cutting. In the past, the tendency was to plant shorter decorative flowers alongside cabbage and other crops.

Whether the style actually originated in France is hard to say, but the most famous potager garden is found at Château de Villandry in the Loire Valley. This particular garden was started in its current form in the early twentieth century and covers around 2.5 acres (1 hectare). However, there have been gardens on this site since the castle was built in 1536.

It's not wrong to say that the potager garden emerged from the Renaissance garden, which was known for its straight lines, low hedges of European boxwood, and gravel paths. The fields were often square and divided into smaller symmetrical sections.

In those days, potager gardens were very much showpieces, with everything growing in straight lines and in an orderly manner. The vegetables were there solely for their ornamental value. They weren't used for cooking, because harvesting them would ruin the meticulous pattern.

All that has now changed. People have kitchen gardens precisely because they want flowers *and* edible crops. While the straight lines are still a distinctive feature, the hedges have been replaced with raised beds.

MY OWN KITCHEN GARDEN

I would love a potager garden, but I simply don't have the right space, hence my container kitchen garden. I can't quite claim to have invented this approach, because many others have, of course, grown vegetables in containers before me.

I've seen pictures from parts of India and Africa of people growing vegetables and other crops in buckets, boxes, and cans—in fact, anything that holds soil. I find this very life-affirming. In harsh conditions, there is less room to think about aesthetics and pretty solutions. It is all about survival.

However, when I started work on this book, there wasn't much information out there about growing edible crops in containers. All research builds on previous findings—they say we stand on each other's shoulders. So, while I was interested in what others had done before me, information was a bit sparse, and I had to start virtually from scratch.

Fortunately, after growing and arranging plants in pots for many years, I was reasonably well-equipped. I wanted to find a look that was a little different from the style I´m normally known for. It was to be a garden within a garden, a space that was allowed to be a bit funky, a bit like an allotment. I also wanted an urban look. All in a small area of about 323 square feet (30 square meters).

To achieve a more intimate look and delineate the new garden, I put up a fence. Naturally, it made sense for me to choose the fence that, here in Denmark, bears my name. I came across it many years ago in England. Over there, it is sometimes called chestnut fencing, but since it sometimes comes in other types of wood, it is simply now known as "Dalby fencing."

Apart from marking the space, the fencing is also pretty, and it is easy to arrange plants along it in pots and other containers, on small tables, on plant racks, and so on.

Earlier, I described my choice of plant containers in more general terms. In the kitchen garden, I aim for a relatively rustic, not too "fancy" look, because I think this aesthetic works well with herbs.

As such, the potting tables up against the greenhouse have concrete tiles, which I designed myself to complement the galvanized stands. I also designed the tall galvanized stands for peas and beans so that the overall look is coherent.

Having different types of plant furniture is important. The stands provide height, and the potting tables allow you to arrange the plants on various levels, all of which means you can grow plenty of plants in a small space and optimize the way they are displayed.

If I had to name the principles that underlie my methods, the word *repetition* would spring to mind. Repetition provides rhythm and a sense of calm. For example, I often place three "subjects" next to each other. This might mean that the plants and the pots are identical. Or perhaps the pots are the same, but the plants are different. Or the plants are the same, but they are planted in three different pots.

I group plants because the garden doesn't look as good if they clash. I also avoid containers that are too small. They impede plant growth and make the garden look too busy.

I don't just grow beans to eat them. Their flowers are beautiful too. This is the runner bean 'Scarlet Emperor'.

FLOWERS IN THE KITCHEN GARDEN

Grow various flowers to add a splash of color between the vegetables. One common feature of these flowers is that they're edible, so you can use them, for example, as a garnish on a salad. One exception is the sweet pea, *Lathyrus*—people often assume it is edible, but it isn't.

Another common feature of many of the flowers in my vegetable garden is that they are orange, such as nasturtiums and marigolds. The good thing about these two plants is that they are easy to sow and grow in pots. If you have a greenhouse, it's best to start there, preferably in March. If you're planting in the open air, wait until April.

It takes about ten to twelve weeks from sowing seeds in the greenhouse to flowers appearing, and a little longer if you sow outdoors. Be aware that marigolds take a bit more time to grow. That's why it's better to start them in a greenhouse or grow them from nursery transplants.

Sow your nasturtiums and marigolds in potting soil without adding nutrients. Use either seed-starting mix or potting soil that you used the year before. It's best to sow these seeds in low-nutrient soil, because fertilizer makes the plants shoot up too fast, which means they use their energy to grow foliage at the expense of flowers. Some types of marigolds need a little more in the way of nutrients.

Nasturtiums

Both the flowers and the tender, round leaves of the nasturtium can be used in salads. They taste similar to cress, and the plant is sometimes known as "monk's cress." You can also pickle nasturtium seeds and eat them like capers.

The plants sometimes look a little sad in summer. When this happens, I clip them down to approximately 4 inches (10 cm) above the ground. It then takes only a few days for them to grow again. After a month or so, they are back in full bloom with fresh buds and flowers.

Pot marigolds are among the easiest of summer flowers. You just have to sow them and wait. They take a few months to bloom.

Pot Marigolds

One of the best things about pot marigolds, also called calendula, is the citrusy scent left on your fingers by the stems and leaves. I notice it every time I cut them for a bouquet, a salad, or a cake. For a cake, you need only a light sprinkling of petals, as they taste slightly spicy. Try making tea from them as well—just pour boiling water over fresh or dried petals and steep for five to ten minutes.

Another idea is to make herb butter. Mix the orange petals with very soft butter, roll it out on baking paper, and place in the fridge. Once the butter is hard, cut the most beautiful slices.

Don't be afraid to cut the flowers—not just calendula, but other summer flowers too. The more flowers you cut, the more they will grow back again. By removing the flowers, you prevent the plant from producing seeds, which is the whole point of the flowers in the first place. When you cut off the flowers, the plant diverts more energy into growing new ones, because it needs to produce more seeds for the species to survive. The same thing happens when you cut nasturtiums back to the ground.

Marigolds

Many people love to hate marigolds. It has been that way ever since they became popular border plants in the 1970s. They went out of fashion for a long time but are now making a comeback, and deservedly so, as there are so many pretty species and varieties.

The marigolds that were so ubiquitous back then were the short ones available in nurseries and garden centers. Sadly, they were often sprayed with a growth-stunting hormone to stop them from taking up too much space in transit to the stores. The taller the plant, the fewer per batch, the higher the shipping fees, the higher the retail prices.

I grow a number of different species that look a bit wilder and more natural than the small border plants of the 1970s.

First, I want to highlight *Tagetes tenuifolia*, which has small flowers and the finest foliage. Two of its varieties are called 'Lemon Gem', which has yellow flowers, and 'Tangerine Gem', which has orange flowers. You might know them as lemon and orange gem marigolds.

Tagetes tenuifolia 'Tangerine Gem', is known as the orange gem marigold. It produces multiple beautiful flowers.

Another beautiful variety is *Tagetes linnaeus,* which originated in the Uppsala garden of Carl Linnaeus (1707–1778) and is named after the famous Swedish botanist.

Linnaeus invented the ingenious Latin naming system that we still use today. Once you understand the plant Latin system, it's easy and indispensable for international communication.

The last species I would like to mention at this point is the African marigold, *Tagetes erecta,* which grows huge pompom-like flowers. It comes in different varieties, but the one I grow is called 'Kees' Orange'. You can use both the petals and foliage, but sparingly. Like pot marigolds, the flavor can be quite overpowering.

Tagetes linnaeus, which is decorative both on the plate and n bouquets. Below right is the African marigold, *Tagetes erecta* 'Kees' Orange'.

PLANTS

GREAT PLANTS FOR BEGINNERS

As you read on, you'll discover that some plants are harder to grow than others. I always advise newcomers to kitchen gardening and container growing to start with some of the easier ones. There are plenty to choose from, and once you're hooked, you'll find no shortage of more challenging projects.

That's how I got started. I knew absolutely nothing when I took up gardening a quarter of a century ago. It has been very much about *learning by doing*, and I've passed on much of what I have learned in numerous books.

I've run into all kinds of problems, and no doubt I still make mistakes. After all, that's how we learn. But occasional successes are important. Success fuels our dreams and gives us the courage to try something more challenging.

Unless you're incredibly ambitious, you don't need grow lights and all sorts of gardening equipment at first. Later on, I would definitely encourage you to try your hand at growing from seed. Watching seeds sprout and grow is simply fascinating.

You can sow so many different seeds in pots. Radishes are the easiest and therefore the most obvious place to start. They are the fastest to grow—just a month from seed to plate.

You can also grow carrots, peas, spinach, and squash in pots. In fact, you can grow spinach and squash in the same one. The spinach will be ready to eat before the squash plants fill out.

In spring, you can buy trays of young plants, ranging from lettuce to leeks and cabbage, at nurseries and garden centers. Don't miss out on the fun of growing lettuce. It's a very hardy plant, and it's difficult to go wrong.

Readers will also discover that you can use pots to grow more than just plants that sprout from seeds. Rhubarb, strawberries, berry bushes, and fruit trees, for instance, are relatively easy to cultivate. They just need the right size container, water, and fertilizer.

Last, but by no means least, I would also encourage you to try growing potatoes in pots or other containers. It really is magical how a single tuber can multiply into so many more.

POTATOES

There's nothing better than freshly harvested potatoes. I think most people would agree with that, even though consumption has fallen significantly in recent years. When I was a child (I was born in 1963), we ate potatoes almost every day. When autumn came, we received a large sack sent by train from my grandparents in the countryside. They were farmers and grew lots of potatoes in the sandy soil of West Jutland.

My grandparents, and a few generations before them, were raised on potatoes. You might think we've been eating potatoes for centuries, but they didn't become commonplace until the mid-eighteenth century. They arrived in Denmark in the 1760s, when Frederik V invited German families to farm the heath in Jutland. People called the newcomers "potato Germans" because of their choice of crop. At first, potatoes were mostly found in the kitchens of the upper classes. Ordinary people took a long time to embrace them, perhaps because they didn't realize you had to boil them. In those days, most Danes lived on oatmeal.

Once people were more familiar with it, the potato soon became an indispensable staple.

In 1918, the Nutrition Council published two hundred thousand copies of the pamphlet titled *Respect the Potato, Grow the Potato* (*Agt paa Kartoflen, dyrk Kartoflen*). The introduction says, "It is the potato that will prevent famine in Europe [...] We begin in deepest seriousness, beset by an agonizing fear, to look for means to avert the distress that threatens [...] One of the last—perhaps the very last—means is and will remain the potato. A nation with a reasonable-sized potato crop in relation to the population will not be afflicted by famine."

The local councils couldn't buy enough potatoes from local farmers, so the government encouraged everybody to grow potatoes on every available patch of land so that as many Danes as possible would be self-sufficient.

Local and county councils were required to use public land for this purpose, but the state had no power over the use of private land, so it could only encourage the owners to grow potatoes. In some places, public land was set aside for allotments. In others, the local authority leased private land and made it available to local people as potato fields. In Copenhagen, the commons were divided into plots for locals to grow their own. Potatoes were also to be grown on military land, where suitable. Land owned by the railways was also used, and unemployed people grew potatoes along the tracks. There was no shortage of ideas.

The growing process

Luckily, potatoes are very easy to grow in pots or buckets. You can buy seed potatoes tested for viruses and bacteria at nurseries and garden centers starting in very early spring. Grown in special fields and sorted and selected according to quality, these seed potatoes lower the risk of plant diseases.

If you want early potatoes, look for varieties like 'Dark Red Norland', 'Yukon Gold', 'Red Cloud', and 'Caribe'. Fingerling potatoes are another option, including 'Rose Finn Apple' and 'Russian Banana'.

In Denmark, we have a variety called the *aspargeskartoffel*, or the asparagus potato. It is a unique potato with a beautiful golden color and a delicate nutty flavor. It is also firm and keeps its shape during cooking. Maybe its name comes from the elongated shape, or maybe it's because they are so delicate. If you have the patience to remove the skin after boiling, they're extra delicious. Definitely don't peel them before cooking. I much prefer to cook them with the skin on. It is similar to a fingerling potato in the United States, which would make a good alternative.

Finding fingerling seed potatoes can be a bit tricky, but it's definitely worth keeping an eye out. If you come across them, strike while the iron is hot!

No matter what variety you grow, it is a good idea to presprout potatoes. I do it in my greenhouse from early March. Place them in an egg tray or similar container with the "eyes" facing upward—that's where the sprouts will emerge. If you don't have a greenhouse, use a windowsill in a bright room that isn't too warm: 59°F to 61°F (approximately 15°C) is ideal. It usually takes about a month before the sprouts are visible. The potatoes are ready to plant when the sprouts are roughly 3/8 inch (1 cm) long.

Take a pot that is 12 inches (30 cm) tall and roughly the same diameter. Fill it halfway with potting soil, and place a potato on top, with the sprouts facing upward. Water well and add more soil, leaving about 4 inches (10 cm) to the top of the pot. Then water again. Don't fill the pot all the way to the brim, because you'll need to add more soil later on to prevent the potatoes from turning green, the same way that we "hill" them in fields.

When the green foliage rises above the rim of the pot, it's time to add more soil and water. Keep the soil moist, but avoid overwatering.

It usually takes about three months before the first potatoes are ready to pick. If you presprout them in early March and plant them in pots roughly a month later, the first ones will be ready in July. You'll know it's time when the flowers start to wither; however, not all varieties produce flowers.

RADISHES

Nothing else is as easy to grow as a radish, except possibly cress. When the spring weather has just warmed, it takes only about three weeks from sowing radish seeds to harvesting crisp radishes. I don't know of any other edible crops that develop so quickly. It's absolutely enchanting.

Denmark is one of the few countries in the world lucky enough to grow radishes in its national colors (red and white). Or so I thought until I heard the Swedes were about to follow suit! The University of Lund informed the Swedish newspaper *Göteborgs-Posten* that seeds for a new genetically modified radish that was blue on the outside and yellow inside, a variety called 'Karl Gustav', would soon be available from Swedish seed companies. I was intrigued and started Googling. I was a bit puzzled that I couldn't find any trace of these new Swedish radishes until I checked the source of the story again and saw the article had been published on April 1, April Fool's Day!

I don't know whether we'll eventually get a radish that reflects the Swedish flag, but they certainly come in colors other than red and white—for example, completely white, pink, and purple.

Some people find the slightly peppery taste of radishes too strong. The distinctive taste is most prominent in summer crops, whereas the early and late crops have a slightly milder taste, especially if watered well and harvested while still very young.

Thinly sliced radishes add a beautifully decorative finishing touch to a salad, and that alone is a good enough reason to grow them. They taste particularly good in a potato salad with freshly harvested peas and beans.

Like all other vegetables, if you don't harvest radishes in time, they will start to flower and set seed. The green seed pods—known as "siliques"—are edible too. They have a crisp texture and are delicious in a salad.

Top: It's pure magic! Sprinkle some seeds in a pot, and you will have crisp radishes in under a month.

Bottom: There are countless varieties of radishes in different shapes and colors. At the top is 'Poloneza', in the middle, 'French Breakfast', and at the bottom, 'Diana'.

The Growing Process

Growing radishes in midsummer can be a bit of an uphill struggle. Not only does the taste become extra sharp, but the radishes also bolt very quickly and start to flower. My advice is to sow them in early spring. I sow them in pots in the greenhouse around March 1, but you can start even earlier. Radish seeds germinate at around 40°F (5°C). To harvest them regularly throughout the spring, I sow my radishes every two weeks until May.

Sow the seeds individually, a couple of inches (a few centimeters) apart. As they grow, harvest every second one to give the others extra space.

'Diana' is a decorative radish variety that tastes the same as the common red-and-white radish, but it looks particularly beautiful in a salad bowl.

RHUBARB

Rhubarb is one of the easiest plants to grow in a container kitchen garden. It is a fairly early crop. If you place the container in the greenhouse in early spring, you can harvest the first tender stalks in early April.

If you want a steady supply of rhubarb throughout the season, it makes sense to plant three varieties with different harvest times.

'Timperley Early' is a well-known and popular variety. It is often recommended because it grows early in the season but also because of its relatively low oxalic acid content. It is the oxalic acid that puts some people off rhubarb because it leaves a fuzzy coating on their teeth.

Another well-known variety is strawberry rhubarb, which is characterized by fairly thin red stalks and is harvested medium-early.

True to their names, 'Canada Red' and 'Crimson Red' are bright varieties also often recommended. The same applies to 'Valentine', which is noted for its low acid.

The Growing Process

Rhubarb is quite easy to grow and thrives in pots with a diameter of 13 to 16 inches (35 to 40 cm). It pays to buy large plants because they establish themselves quite quickly. But don't harvest them in the first year, and more generally, resist the urge to harvest too many stalks. In year two, only harvest about a quarter at a time.

Ease the stalks out gently so that the light-colored end comes with them. This lets new stalks grow. When cleaning rhubarb in the kitchen, be sure not to cut off the light-colored end. It's the most flavorsome part.

Water your rhubarb well. It is a productive, fast-growing plant, so it needs added nutrients. In spring, I sprinkle composted chicken manure around the base. Once I have harvested all of the stalks, I give each plant another handful or two.

Forcing Rhubarb

You can get an early crop of rhubarb by placing the pot in the greenhouse in early spring. Another solution—and quite an attractive one—is to use a rhubarb cloche. More commonly known as rhubarb forcers, they were popular in England in Victorian times, and you still see them in kitchen gardens there. They have become popular in other countries as well, particularly because they are so decorative, but they're also highly practical.

Place the forcer over the plant in early spring, and leave it out in the sun. The terra cotta heats up, bringing the plant to life, and the stalks start to grow. When they are long enough, they start to lift the lid, and that means it's time to harvest.

A forcer gets the plant off to a quick start and helps it grow extra-long stalks, and the lack of light makes the stalks less acidic.

ASPARAGUS

I don't remember exactly when I first heard about green asparagus, but it must have been a good twenty years ago. Before that, I knew only the white version, and even then, only the kind that came in jars and tins. I was completely unaware that you could grow asparagus yourself.

Nowadays, both fresh green and white asparagus are delicacies on par with new potatoes when they are ready in early May. It used to be a matter of eating as many spears as possible before the season ended around midsummer, but fresh green asparagus is now on sale all year round. These imported varieties are slightly smaller and more delicate, and you can use them in various dishes. However, like strawberries, I use asparagus only when it is in season. I would never dream of buying it in winter or even summer.

The reason why the end of the asparagus season is so crucial is that harvesting after midsummer exhausts the plants. The asparagus keeps growing after that, but it needs to shoot up and mature into its fern-like foliage. This is essential for ensuring photosynthesis and nourishing the roots. We do the same with tulip stems so they produce flowers the following year.

You will love the beautiful plants. They are about 3 feet (1 m) high, with needle-like leaves and delicate little yellow-green flowers, which are later replaced by lacquer-red berries on female plants. It is tempting to cut those flowering shoots and use them in bouquets, but resist the temptation. Leave the shoots standing for the winter.

Speaking of beautiful foliage, some varieties of asparagus are grown for decorative purposes—as potted plants and for cutting for use as greenery in bouquets.

Hanging asparagus has become a popular potted plant in recent years. Another type of asparagus known as "bridal veil" has fine green foliage that is commonly used in bouquets. These are different species than edible asparagus.

The Growing Process

Asparagus grows very well in a pot without other plants or weeds. It doesn't like competition.

Budding asparagus growers need to be patient. Starting from seed takes a long time—three to four years from sowing to harvest—although you can buy pregrown plants to save time.

Asparagus seeds need a relatively high temperature to germinate, around 77°F (25°C). This means you can sow them indoors in March. Once the green shoots emerge, move the plants to the greenhouse, where there is more light and heat. Later, when the plants are ready to be handled, move them to medium-size pots. You can repot them again during the summer. Three is a suitable number of plants in a pot with a diameter of approximately 16 inches (40 cm). It will be at least three seasons before you can start harvesting the asparagus, and don't expect much of a yield in the first year. For the first harvest, it is best to pick the spears for only one week.

I've read that even plants over twenty years old can be highly productive when well-established in the ground outdoors. How long you can grow asparagus in containers remains to be seen. So far, I've enjoyed a couple of seasons with a good crop.

As mentioned, you can get a head start by buying pregrown plants, either bareroot or potted. You can harvest them just one year after planting, but ideally you should wait two seasons. It pays off in the long run. Bare-root plants go on sale in early spring.

Spread the roots out well, and cover with approximately 2 inches (5 cm) of topsoil. If you have access to seaweed, it is a good idea to place a layer over the topsoil. Asparagus grows naturally in coastal areas and is often covered by washed-up seaweed. It is native to warm and temperate regions of southern Europe, Asia Minor, and North Africa, where it prefers riverbanks. It is often spread via bird droppings after the birds have eaten the berries. This does not affect the germination of the seeds.

GREEN AND WHITE ASPARAGUS

White asparagus is considered the most desirable, but I prefer green asparagus and its slightly pea-like flavor. The delicate green color adds some visual interest to your plate. When boiling green asparagus, it is extremely important not to cook it for more than a minute.

When planting, it doesn't matter which color you like best, because the color—or lack thereof—is determined by how you treat the plants. If you stop them from being exposed to sunlight, the spears will be pale. This usually means piling up soil around the shoots, but this is a little difficult to do in a pot. Another option is to cover them with a bucket or possibly a rhubarb cloche (see page 89).

White asparagus is often thicker than green and also coarser, so it needs to be peeled. It also needs to be boiled for longer, typically up to five minutes, depending on thickness.

LETTUCE

Growing lettuce is easy and rewarding, which makes it ideal for beginners. The fresh leaves, which you can harvest throughout the season, are much tastier and crisper than anything on sale in a shop. Lettuce in pots is incredibly decorative, even if you are unlucky and they bolt. They may not be very useful in the kitchen if that happens, but you can still enjoy the flowers.

Lettuce is a frugal plant when it comes to soil and nutrients. There are so many lovely varieties, with deeply lobed, smooth, and curly leaves. I find the dark leaves particularly beautiful in both the garden and the salad bowl.

Generally speaking, there are two types of lettuce: leaf lettuce, which is harvested as loose leaves, and head lettuce, which, as the name suggests, forms heads.

It is easy to sow a seed mixture of baby greens in a pot. Harvest the leaves, which might also include arugula, spinach, and chard, while young. The first tender leaves are ready to pick after about a month. Harvesting them thins out the plants, leaving the remaining ones more room to grow.

While you can sow baby greens relatively close together, head lettuce needs space, so either thin them out or move the plants to individual pots with a diameter of around 6 inches (15 cm) or larger pots with approximately 8 inches (20 cm) between each plant. At first, the plants don't take up much space, but the heads slowly start to take shape. They are ready to harvest two to three months after sowing.

Lettuce leaves aren't particularly nutritious or filling, but they are an indispensable part of summer cuisine.

Lettuce isn't just a spring and summer crop. You can grow lettuce in late summer, autumn, and well into winter. The plants may look quite delicate, but they can easily withstand a few degrees of frost. Be careful, though—a damp winter can rot lettuce, so you may want to cover it.

As well as lettuce, I have chosen to include spinach and common purslane in this section, as both are leafy vegetables perfect for salads.

The Growing Process

As mentioned, lettuce is quite easy to grow as long as you bear one thing in mind: the seeds may be reluctant to germinate if it is too warm. The optimum temperature is 50°F to 59°F (10°C to 15°C), which means it will take only a few days for green shoots to appear. I sow mine in March in the greenhouse. Later in the season, I pre-cultivate lettuce outdoors. It's best that the temperature doesn't exceed 68°F (20°C).

I sow in trays and transplant the small plants into individual pots, where I leave them to grow a little before moving them into larger pots and containers.

As mentioned, lettuce requires little in the way of nutrition to thrive, so you can grow it in potting soil used for other crops.

If, like me, you like leafy plants with beautiful colors, you'll love growing lettuce. There are so many varieties with different shades. My favorites are the dark-leaved varieties, which I grow in containers and beds.

LEAF LETTUCE

The great thing about leaf lettuce is that you can harvest it bit by bit. It grows in a rosette formation, so if you harvest the leaves from the bottom and always leave some at the top, new leaves will grow. This is especially true in spring and summer, when the plants grow well. In autumn, the lettuce grows more slowly, so don't expect a big postseason harvest.

HEAD LETTUCE

It's almost like magic. In just two or three months, a few loose leaves sprouting from a root form a dense head, comprising a rosette of large, green outer leaves and a light-green core. A lettuce head looks a bit like a large double rose with plenty of petals.

One of my childhood memories is my grandma's green salad tossed in a dressing made from heavy whipping cream, lemon juice, and sugar—"grandma's dressing." In the summer, we often enjoyed this salad on Sundays, served with pot-roasted chicken stuffed with parsley.

ARUGULA

About twenty years ago, arugula became very popular in foodie circles and was used in almost everything, which was a bit too much of a good thing. It has a sharp and slightly peppery taste that mixes well with other leaves in a salad, which is why I grow it. Note that there is also a wild arugula. Unlike the common variety, it is perennial.

In spring, I grow arugula as baby leaves, and because of its distinctive flavor, I use it almost like an herb. In summer, arugula flowers quickly, and flea beetles often attack, taking tiny bites out of the leaves. The beetles appear in May to June, so I wait until July to sow a new batch.

The plants will then grow over the late summer, so you can harvest in early autumn. If you harvest earlier, leave the bottom 2 inches (5 cm) of the rosette to allow new leaves to sprout.

LAMB'S LETTUCE

This small lettuce with a rosette of juicy green leaves looks rather delicate but is surprisingly hardy. It can easily withstand a normal cold-climate winter, remaining fresh and green during the dark months right through to early spring.

The small, aromatic leaves add much-needed lift to a salad, or you can use them as a garnish. The flavor is initially slightly spicy and a bit nutty. Later, it becomes more bitter but remains delicate. Snip the leaves without stripping the whole plant, and fresh foliage will shoot up.

SPINACH

You might be thinking, "That's not a lettuce!" but I've included it here because I like to use the green leaves in mixed salads, especially the small baby leaves. You can also use spinach in hot dishes, but it's almost a pity to do so, because the leaves wilt and almost disappear in a pan or wok.

Spinach is very easy to grow, and you can sow the first batch as early as March. The seeds sprout quickly, even when the soil is only a few degrees above freezing—39°F to 41°F (4°C to 5°C) is enough. Sowing early is definitely an advantage, because when the temperature rises, the plants often bolt and flower. That's why it's difficult to grow spinach in the summer. I sow it again in August so I have fresh leaves throughout the fall. You can also sow even later and harvest in early spring. Spinach plants tolerate quite a bit of frost. As the weather gradually warms up, spinach plants grow rapidly.

I sow and harvest the baby spinach bit by bit and leave some plants to mature. Ideally, leave about 6 inches (15 cm) between them. If you haven't grown spinach before, it's definitely worth a try. Homegrown leaves are far more flavorful than anything in supermarkets. There's just no comparison.

It's a good idea to sow spinach along with squash. Squash doesn't take much room, at first, so you can use the space for early spinach.

COMMON PURSLANE

Here's another crop that isn't strictly speaking a lettuce leaf, but you can use it in the same way.

Common purslane is a decorative, fleshy plant with shiny, succulent, and crisp leaves and fresh shoots you can eat raw in salads. It tastes a bit like snow peas—in other words, it's really delicious! I sow the fine seeds in May when no more frosts are expected. Once they sprout, I transplant the seedlings into smaller cells in plant trays and later into pots, spaced approximately 4 inches (10 cm) apart.

When the shoots are approximately 2 inches (5 cm) high, cut them for the first time an inch or so (a few centimeters) above the ground. Soon the plants will branch out, and you can harvest them again and again.

I have read that common purslane is a bit sensitive to temperature, so it might be a good idea to keep it in a greenhouse. Having said that, mine thrive outdoors all summer.

BELGIAN ENDIVE

Endive plays an important role in my winter cooking, just as pointed cabbage (also known as sweetheart cabbage) does in the summer. It has a distinctive flavor and is delicious in salads. It is also wonderful halved, baked in the oven, and garnished with butter and Parmesan.

The growing process is a bit time-consuming and labor-intensive but incredibly fascinating. I highly recommend that you give it a go, because it will help you learn to grow indoors during the winter.

'Brussels Witloof' is an old variety that has been grown since the mid-nineteenth century. It develops large, broad, dandelion-like leaves over the summer. They have the slightly bitter flavor characteristic of chicory leaves. The roots grow during summer, and it's important to make them as strong as possible, because this means more leaves and, ultimately, a stronger head.

To harvest in winter, sow the seeds as early as May. It is best to sow in a tray with small cells so you don't disturb the roots when transplanting. This will make the roots stronger. Gradually move to larger pots, as explained earlier, until they end up in one that isn't too shallow and has a diameter of approximately 8 inches (20 cm).

In late autumn, cut the leaves an inch or so (a few centimeters) above the soil surface. Then move the pot to a room with a temperature of around 50°F (10°C), and cover it with a bucket or similar to block out the light. After a week, place the pot in a slightly warmer spot, around 59°F to 68°F (15°C to 20°C). Water sparingly as fresh leaves sprout. After about three weeks, a fine head will form and it is time to harvest.

If you want to grow more, dig out some roots, place them side by side in a pot, and move them to a greenhouse. You can plant them quite close together.

RADICCHIO

With its slightly bitter taste and decorative red leaves, radicchio is a real autumn lettuce. I sow it in June. Radicchio grows quite slowly, so it takes a while for the heads to form. At first, the leaves are green, but they slowly change to their characteristic deep red, which beautifully matches the burnt colors of autumn. When harvesting the heads, cut them off at ground level instead of uprooting the whole plant. That way, there is a chance of fresh leaves growing. It depends on how late you harvest.

Finely chopped radicchio, mixed with nuts and apple slices and tossed in oil and vinegar dressing, is a real delicacy. I like to add other leaves in different colors, because radicchio can be a little too bitter on its own.

Radicchio is particularly popular in Italy, where it is used in risotto and panfried in olive oil and garlic.

Nowadays, you can buy all kinds of produce all year round, but radicchio is an exception. It usually doesn't appear on sale until fall but is then available all winter. It's nice to have some delicious, seasonal produce during the darker months.

Top: At one point, I was lucky enough to find some nice old wine barrels that had been cut in half and are perfect for growing lettuce. I also use them for peas and beans, which grow tall as they climb iron frames.

Bottom: This is the 'Rosa di Verona' variety, which I plant outdoors in early September. The photo, opposite, was taken a few weeks later. Here, the heads are beginning to take shape.

CARROTS

Growing carrots is so easy. Don't deny yourself the pleasure! They also grow quickly, which means that if you sow early, you can grow another crop in the same pot. It's important to note that there are both summer and winter carrots. I always grow the former, because they develop faster. Carrots grown in autumn and winter have a much coarser texture. I prefer the tender summer ones.

There are many different varieties, not only in terms of size but also color. In addition to the common orange varieties, there are also white, yellow, purple, and red carrots. The white and yellow varieties have a slightly milder flavor than the orange ones, while purple carrots have a slightly spicy taste. But these are subtle differences. The main reason I grow the different colors is that they look so attractive.

The Growing Process

You can harvest early carrots in late May if you sow them in a greenhouse in mid-March. Sow in a pot that is at least 12 inches (30 cm) high. Carrots are root vegetables, so they need to be sowed in soil and not transplanted. Sprinkle the

seeds thinly, which is easier when they are mixed with a little sand, and cover with a thin layer of soil.

When they sprout and are ready to be handled, thin out the seedlings, leaving 1.2 to 1.6 inches (3 to 4 cm) between them. Then, wait two or three weeks and harvest every second carrot. The young ones are small and delicate and make really delicious snacks. After a month or so, the remaining carrots will be ready to harvest.

It goes without saying that you can also thin out the plants right from the beginning and start with them 2.4 to 3.1 inches (6 to 8 cm) apart. It just means that you miss out on enjoying the young carrots.

Many people who have tried growing carrots in their garden are all too familiar with the carrot fly, which lays eggs on the surface of the soil. After just a week or two, larvae appear, attack the carrots, and eat holes in them. I've been lucky to avoid these pesky pests. I have raised my pots 3 feet (1 m) or so above ground, as I'd heard that the flies prefer to stay near the ground. Although I haven't been able to confirm this, my carrots have been free from attacks.

PEAS

Fresh peas are as much of a delicacy as new potatoes. They taste best straight from the pod, but their sweet crispness is also unrivaled in salads and other dishes. Frozen peas just don't compare.

There are plenty of good reasons to grow your own peas, especially because you can pick them as you need them. If you buy a bag of peas from the grocer, you'll often find that some of them are the size of pinheads. That is because the producer picked them all at once—ripe or not.

Peas come in numerous varieties that differ in terms of their height and the color of their pods. The purple pods are particularly beautiful, although the peas themselves are green.

If you want to add some color to your salad bowl, I recommend purple snow peas or sugar snap peas. Snow peas, which have flat pods, are harvested before the peas inside develop, so it is the crunchy pods that we eat. Sugar snap peas, which are a cross between ordinary peas and snow peas, also have edible pods, but unlike snow peas, you only harvest them once the peas inside have developed. They have thicker pods than snow peas.

In the UK and Europe, a common name for sugar snap peas and snow peas is *mangetout*, a French phrase that means "eat everything."

Top: 'Oregon Sugar Pod' is a delicate snow pea picked while the pods are completely flat and before the peas develop. It is delicious fresh in a salad but also good stir-fried in a pan.

Bottom: 'Opal Creek' is easy to recognize due to its subtle cream-yellow color. Again, both the pods and the peas are edible.

Opposite Top and Bottom Left: The 'Blauwschokker' pea has edible purple pods and green peas. It is important to harvest them regularly. If you wait too long, the peas become mealy and the pods too coarse.

Opposite Bottom Right: The bush pea 'Half Pint' (known in the US as 'Tom Thumb') is a small, compact variety.

The Growing Process

Sow in pots or seed trays, outdoors and in the greenhouse. To speed up the sprouting process, soak the seeds in water for about twelve hours before sowing them.

Outdoors, sow from mid-March to mid-June. In the greenhouse, you can start in early March. Not only does growing in the greenhouse mean you can harvest peas early, but it also stops birds and mice from eating the tender plants.

Bush peas, which only grow to a height of around $1^1/_2$ feet (45 cm), do well in pots with a diameter of 10 to 12 inches (25 to 30 cm), with five to seven plants in each. Use canes to support the stems. I grow tall peas on cone-shaped racks in half wine barrels with a distance of about 4 inches (10 cm) between the plants.

Peas make a good starter plant for children. They are easy to grow and do so quite quickly (little ones can be a bit impatient!), and most children love them. Low bush peas are particularly good because they literally grow at a child's eye level. There are a number of different varieties, and my two favorites are 'Half Pint' ('Tom Thumb') and 'Desiree'. The latter has beautiful dark pods.

'Half Pint'/'Tom Thumb', shown in the pictures on the next page, is a nineteenth-century heirloom variety.

TOMATOES

Tomatoes have become the most widely grown vegetable garden plant by far, and interest in special varieties with different sizes, colors, and flavors has steadily increased. Seed companies now offer an extensive selection, and nurseries and garden centers have also broadened their ranges. The era of only a few red varieties of tomatoes is long gone.

I grow tomatoes because I enjoy it, and I have the right conditions—artificial lighting and a greenhouse—although that's mostly because I can't resist. It's much easier to buy garden-ready plants, and the good news is that there are many nurseries that offer a wide selection of tomato varieties.

Types of Tomato

Tomatoes used to be round and red, at least in supermarkets. The selection is better these days, but it still doesn't begin to approach the variety you can grow yourself. The sheer diversity is quite amazing. The different varieties and species of tomatoes range from tiny ones (called currant tomatoes) to really big beefsteaks, which are good in stews or stuffed and topped with a gratin.

The slightly elongated plum tomatoes are often found in supermarkets, still on the stem and complete with leaves. I am sure that many of us are attracted by the greenery! It reminds me of how lemons with the leaves still on have found their way into stores in recent seasons. They serve as an extra reminder that these are natural products—just in case we'd forgotten!

Cherry tomatoes are also worth a mention. They are small but slightly bigger than currant tomatoes. The next size up is the cocktail tomato and then standard or globe tomatoes, which are still the most widely grown.

Please note that these types are a rough classification, as the terms are somewhat fluid.

Tomatoes vary in size and color. They can be cream colored, light yellow, warm yellow, orange, purple, pink, or even almost black. You even get tomatoes that are green when ripe, although the term "green tomatoes" usually refers to unripe ones, which taste really good when pickled.

The different colors are all absolutely fascinating, as you can see from the pictures in this section. I grow most of them.

Top: 'Sungold'
Bottom 'Chocolate Cherry'
Opposite Bottom Left: 'White Beauty'
Opposite Bottom Right: 'Black Beauty'

The Growing Process

Tomatoes aren't difficult to grow, but you need to start quite early. I sow mine under grow lights in early March. You can start even earlier if you have the right equipment, such as grow lights and maybe a heating mat.

Seeds

It's pretty easy to build up your own supply of tomato seeds. Cut a fully ripe tomato in half and use the tip of a knife to transfer seeds to a piece of paper towel or a coffee filter. Put the paper somewhere warm so the seeds dry. The slimy pulp around the seeds will stick to the paper. You can cut the paper away, but you don't have to—it won't stop the seeds from germinating.

Seeds taken from specially bred varieties, known as F1 hybrids, are less predictable. If you want to grow these varieties, I recommend buying seeds.

Sowing

Sow the seeds in small trays at a temperature of around 68°F (20°C). In a few days, small green shoots will start to appear. You can sow tomato seeds at lower temperatures, but they will take longer to sprout.

Once the plants are ready to be handled, repot them in gradually larger medium-size pots. Leave only the top of the plant visible.

Containers

The most common method of growing tomatoes is to use grow bags placed on capillary boxes (self-watering planters) made of polystyrene. The boxes are useful because you don't need to fill them with water as often. About once every two weeks will do for a couple of plants, which means you can go away for days at a time without worrying about them. The downside is that they don't look great.

I have swapped my grow bags and capillary boxes for more attractive 12- to 14-inch (30 to 35 cm) pots. My tomatoes thrive in them. There is room for more soil, and the soil I use is better quality.

One minor problem with pots is that you need to water the tomato plants more often than you do in capillary boxes. I am lucky to have help with all my pots.

Support

Most types of tomato plants can easily grow to over 6 feet (2 m) in height, so they need support. In greenhouses, it is common to use string, specially designed hangers, or similar. I don't really like dangling tomato plants, so I tie them to 1/4-inch (6-mm) round iron rods that curve to form a hook at the top. It's an easy, simple, and effective system.

Pinching

If you let ordinary tomato plants grow, they will form a wild "bush" that soon takes up too much space.

As the plant grows taller, side shoots (also known as suckers) appear, which you have to remove regularly, ideally when they're just a few centimeters long and you can do it easily with your fingers. When they are longer and thicker, removing them becomes more difficult and often leaves behind a "stub" that is vulnerable to fungus.

In mid-August, I also pinch off the top of the shoots, because the flowers there—and later, the tomatoes—won't have time to fully develop. Once the flowers have been pollinated, it will take another couple of months for the fruit to ripen. This means they won't be ready until late October, by which time the days are too short and the temperature too low for the tomatoes to ripen.

Removing the top of the shoots means that instead of using energy to flower, the plant focuses on the tomatoes that have already formed, which will grow larger.

I used the word *ordinary* at the beginning of this section because the most common tomato varieties grow upwards. However, bush/pot/patio tomato varieties, which have become popular in recent years, have a dense, bushy growth and don't need to be pinched. Bush tomatoes produce relatively small tomatoes and are, unsurprisingly, really good in pots.

Cuttings

Growing tomatoes from cuttings isn't something you hear about a lot, but it's actually quite simple. You can use the side shoots that you pinch off as cuttings, as long as they are at least 3 to 4 inches (8 to 10 cm) long. You can then plant the cuttings in moist potting soil, as explained on pages 230–231.

Growing Tomatoes Outdoors

You can also grow tomatoes outdoors as long as you have a sunny, south-facing spot and a warm summer. Bush and patio tomatoes grow particularly well outdoors because they are small. Large tomatoes, such as beefsteaks, are another option for growing outdoors, though they take longer to mature. Interestingly, tomatoes grown outdoors often have a more intense flavor than those grown in greenhouses because they ripen more slowly.

Watering

It goes without saying that a 6-foot (2 m)-tall plant with lots of foliage and many tomatoes needs a lot of water. It's still a good idea to let tomato plants go a little dry from time to time. If you overwater a plant, you can "drown" it, as the roots don't get enough oxygen. Holding back a little on watering also gives the fruit more flavor.

Allow the surface of the soil to dry out a little between each watering, but if the leaves start to droop, get the hose or watering can out.

'Ola Polka', a Polish heirloom variety, is a bush tomato that thrives outdoors when the weather is mild and warm. The yellow color really brightens up the garden.

CUCUMBERS

Like tomatoes, cucumbers make great greenhouse plants. I seldom grow ordinary green cucumbers outdoors because I have a greenhouse, but I know many gardeners do, especially in the United States. I have tried growing a special yellow variety outdoors—'Crystal Lemon'. It doesn't look like a cucumber, but when you taste it, there is no doubt. Compared to regular green cucumbers, lemon ones have quite a lot of seeds. I grow it mainly for its decorative value. Instead of training it to grow upwards, I let the vines creep along the fence that surrounds my kitchen garden. The variety of green cucumber known as 'Burpless Tasty Green' is a good choice for outdoor growing.

Cucumbers don't come in as many types as tomatoes. In addition to the above, there are regular salad cucumbers and mini ones, which differ in size but not in taste.

Gherkins have little in common with juicy green cucumbers. Grown outdoors, they are slightly smaller than mini cucumbers and have to be pickled before you can eat them. Finally, there are cucamelons, which I mention for the sake of

It is hard to believe that this round fruit, known as 'Crystal Lemon', is actually a cucumber. But the taste is unmistakable.

completeness. They grow to no more than 1 to 2 inches (2 to 3 cm) in length and look like mini watermelons. Cucamelons are eaten as snacks or used in salads.

If you have a greenhouse or a sunny spot outdoors, grow salad cucumbers and mini cucumbers, because freshly harvested dark-green cucumbers taste much better than the ones you buy, especially if you harvest them before they get too big. They are extra crisp at that stage.

I use cucumbers in salads all summer. I often cut them lengthwise and scrape out the seeds. Cucumber soup is another delicious summer dish; simply blend cucumber and garlic with crème fraîche or similar, and season with salt and pepper.

When cucumbers are plentiful, I make old-fashioned cucumber salad. Slice the cucumber very thinly and place it in a marinade of apple cider vinegar and sugar, along with plenty of freshly ground pepper. It will be ready to serve after an hour or two. To make cucumber salad particularly summery, add a little finely chopped dill.

The Growing Process

Cucumbers require quite a lot of warmth, so don't sow or plant them too early. I usually sow around May 1, perhaps a little later if the weather is cold, after the danger of frost has passed. The temperature must not fall below 68°F (20°C), so it may be a good idea to cover the plants at night.

The roots don't like to be disturbed, so I sow in pots—two seeds in each. That way, you can be fairly sure that at least one of them will sprout. If two plants emerge, remove one by cutting it out rather than pulling so you don't risk damaging the roots of the other plant.

When the plant is about 4 to 6 inches (10 to 15 cm) tall, move it to a pot with a diameter of 12 to 14 inches (30 to 35 cm). Although I use metal poles to support my tomato plants, I don't recommend them for cucumbers, because they tend to slip down. I use a metal chain instead.

If you want a lot of cucumbers, prune the plant. Be harsh at first. Pinch off the first flowers that appear at the top of the main stem to make sure you can harvest throughout the season. Where you remove the flowers, side shoots will develop, which then produce flowers, and later cucumbers. When each of the new shoots has two leaves, pinch them off after the second leaf. New side shoots will quickly appear on the ones you have just pinched. Pinch them off after the second leaf too. Tie the new shoots to the chain as you go, and keep pinching off new shoots, as described above. It is important to be vigilant to prevent the shoots from getting out of control, but pinching off bit by bit is worth it in the long run. New cucumbers will appear all the time, and it's fascinating to see how many you can harvest from a single plant.

CHILIES AND PEPPERS

More and more people are growing their own chilies, as hot dishes are becoming increasingly popular.

I understand the fascination with these small, powerful fruits. Many people grow all sorts of varieties, with varying degrees of heat. Personally, I am not a big fan of growing chilies, mainly because I don't like food that is too spicy. On the other hand, I like the little kick mild chilies give to a dish, so I grow a few varieties.

'Red Habanero' is one of the best-known hot chilies, and it's definitely not for the fainthearted! The hottest chilies come from Mexico, due to the warm climate. Strong chilies need consistently high temperatures. The strength also depends on ripeness and which part of the fruit you use. A chili is mildest at the pointed end and strongest near the stem. The white seed walls and the seed pod on which the seeds sit are the hottest parts.

The strength of a chili is measured using the Scoville scale.

Top: Korean red chili peppers
Bottom: 'Corno di Toro'

Opposite Top: 'Sugar Rush Cream'

Opposite Bottom: 'Chocolate Beauty'

Top. 'Lemon Spice' jalapeño

At the mildest end of the scale, with a Scoville rating of zero, are ordinary bell peppers. I grow these for their beauty and to add a nice crunch to salads. Peppers are particularly delicate and sweet when baked, peeled, and tossed in good olive oil. Stuffed peppers are also a classic dish.

Green peppers used to be the most common. Yellow, orange, and red peppers are now more popular. They have a sweeter and milder taste than the green ones, which are sharper because they're not ripe yet. On the other hand, this means that green peppers have a longer shelf life than the other colors.

Peppers vary in shape too. The most common ones are round and plump, but there are also elongated, pointed peppers, which look almost like enlarged chilies.

The Growing Process

The process of propagating chilies and peppers from seeds is quite similar to that of tomatoes (see page 116), and I sow them at the same time, in early March, at a temperature of around 50°F (10°C). It is always exciting to see which ones will sprout first, although there's usually not much difference.

The plants are transplanted and repotted into gradually larger pots, like tomatoes.

Pests and Useful Insects

For some reason, aphids find chili and pepper plants really attractive, especially when the plants are very young. The aphids suck plant sap from the leaves, causing them to curl up. If the infestation is detected early, you can introduce other insects—such as ladybugs and parasitic wasps—to reduce the aphid population. You can buy them from a company that sells biological pest-control solutions for greenhouses, conservatories, and gardens. The insects take it from there.

To remove aphids from fully grown plants, use insecticidal soap, or just dip the plants in cold water.

Pinching

Pinch off the first buds as soon as they appear. This sounds harsh, but by removing five to ten buds, you encourage the plant to develop and grow larger instead of expending too much energy on growing fruit right from the outset.

Some people choose to pinch off the top shoots of the plants to encourage them to branch out. I don't. If you want the plant to look like a small tree with a trunk, remove the lower leaves once it is established.

Overwintering

Both chilies and peppers can overwinter. As long as they have plenty of light and you keep them at a temperature of 59°F to 77°F (15°C to 20°C), they will retain their foliage. Temperatures down to 50°F (10°C) are also okay, but it will send the plants into a state of dormancy, in which they shed their leaves. This means that you should water them very sparingly. When it gets warmer, the plants will sprout again, at which point you should gradually increase the frequency of watering. The same applies to fertilization.

'Carmagnola Rosso' is a well-known and highly prized pepper with a beautiful red color. It can also be harvested unripe, when it is green.

The chilies and peppers shown in the photos in this section were grown in a greenhouse. I move them outside on warm days.

EGGPLANT

When you use the word *eggplant* as an adjective, most people know you mean the color. It is a very deep and dark purple, almost black. It is also the most common color for the fruit, but you will also find violet, orange, white, and cream varieties with different patterns. As you know, I love color, and I am very fond of eggplant. Their shiny surface and different hues make them particularly interesting to grow.

They are called *eggplant* because the common varieties can, with a little goodwill, be described as egg-shaped, but there are also more elongated and round varieties.

If you have success with tomatoes, chilies, and peppers, you might want to try your hand at eggplants, too, as you grow them the same way.

Eggplant is somewhat underrated. Around the Mediterranean, where it is known as *aubergines*, it is much loved in dishes like ratatouille and moussaka.

You have to be careful when frying eggplant in oil (at least if you want to stay slim), as it soaks up oil like a sponge. I grill slices on a pan, season them, and toss them in a little oil with lemon juice.

Top: 'Farmer's Long' is a slender and impressive variety.
Bottom: 'Rosa Bianca' is beautiful and doesn't look like an ordinary eggplant.

Top: In addition to its beautiful fruit, eggplant also produces the most exquisite flowers. Sadly, it is advisable to remove the first two or three flowers to encourage a more vigorous bush.

Opposite: 'Kaberi' is a variety with fairly small fruits, about the size of a hen's egg.

The Growing Process

Sow and handle your eggplant in the same way as tomatoes (see page 116). However, it likes the heat and prefers a minimum temperature of around 68°F (20°C). If you live in a cooler summer climate like mine, eggplant thrives best in a greenhouse, but during warm periods, I move them outdoors into the kitchen garden, where they look highly decorative. Gardeners with full sun and warm summers can grow them outdoors full-time easily.

As with chilies and peppers, you should remove the first flowers. However, with eggplant, it is enough to pinch off the first two or three buds or flowers to encourage the plant to grow. I am always reluctant to do this, because the blue-purple flowers are so beautiful. But as we know, you can't make an omelet without breaking a few eggs—or eggplant flowers!

When the plant is about 12 inches (30 cm) tall, pinch off the top. This will make the plant branch out. If you want really big eggplant, remove new flowers after the first five or six fruits have formed.

GARLIC

These days, garlic is an essential ingredient in my kitchen, right up there with onions. Especially in winter, when I stir-fry most of my vegetables or bake them in the oven, garlic is a must.

The use of garlic in Danish cuisine really took off in the 1960s, when we developed a taste for Mediterranean food and pasta dishes. In North America, garlic has long been a favorite ingredient in Italian and other ethnic communities, particularly in large cities. Garlic is also a fundamental part of the culinary DNA in countries like Spain, Italy, and France.

When I was growing up, garlic just didn't appear on the menu. The first time I saw it in a recipe, it told me to rub the inside of a salad bowl with a clove. You didn't want it to be too overpowering, after all! People used to worry about garlic breath, including me. I sometimes ask people if I smell like it. So far, the answer has always been no. But then again, maybe they're just being polite.

As far as we know, the smell usually comes from crushed cloves. Finely chopped or minced garlic is thought to be less pungent.

Garlic is quite easy to grow. It just requires a little patience. You should plant cloves as early as October. They quickly establish roots and start to sprout. In a mild fall and winter, green tips may emerge through the soil around December or January. It's a good idea to move the pot into your greenhouse or cover the sprouts with fleece or a similar material if the temperature drops below 37°F to 39°F (3°C to 4°C).

There are two types of garlic—soft-neck and hard-neck. You can braid the soft-neck varieties and hang them up to dry, as they do in southern Europe. The hard-neck types are also called "snake garlic" in Danish, as the top of the stem "snakes" into a decorative arch known as a scape. Small bulblets form at the top of the scape, and you can use them for propagation. But it takes a couple of years before they're ready to eat. I scatter them around the beds in my garden and enjoy the decorative look as they grow.

Some people think it's a good idea to cut off the scapes, along with 6 to 8 inches (15 to 20 cm) of the stem around midsummer. This is supposed to stop the plant from wasting energy on forming the bulblets and direct its energy to the garlic bulb under the ground. Others recommend leaving the top as it is. I've tried both methods and noticed little difference.

The twisted stems look beautiful in bouquets, and the green leaves with a distinct garlic flavor can be finely chopped and eaten like chives.

The Growing Process

Every autumn, you can buy beautiful, big seed garlic bulbs online, at well-stocked garden centers, and at nurseries. Divide them into cloves, and place the cloves in the soil with the tip facing upwards, approximately 4 inches (10 cm) apart. Cover with approximately 2 inches (5 cm) of soil, and water well. After that, only water when green shoots appear above the soil. Slowly increase the frequency of watering, but only when the surface is dry. It is important not to overwater, as this can rot the cloves.

Like onions, garlic doesn't need much fertilizer. It's a good idea to cover the soil with a thin layer of compost in early spring or occasionally apply liquid fertilizer.

I've been growing garlic for the last couple of seasons, and it has gone well. Both times, I bought seed garlic online. You can also use regular garlic from a store or supermarket, but they are rarely as big or attractive. Last autumn, I planted cloves from both supermarket garlic and seed garlic. It will be fascinating to see the results this summer. My guess is that the supermarket garlic will be a little smaller but probably still quite good.

The most important thing is that you grow your garlic organically. Conventionally grown garlic and other alliums are often treated with a chemical agent to prevent them from sprouting before you use them in the kitchen.

Harvesting and Drying

In mid-July, it is time to harvest. Try lifting a single bulb to see if it has grown into a collection of cloves. If it has, it is ready. Another sign is that the stems are beginning to thin and wither at the top. However, unlike onions, which are closely related, the stems won't go limp.

Dry the harvested garlic to store for the winter. Remove the tops. There should be around six to eight cloves per bunch. It is important that the bulbs are exposed to air. When it's dry, you can hang them outside in a sunny spot, but if the weather turns wet, it's better to dry them in a greenhouse, under an eave, or on a windowsill for three to four weeks. Cut the stems of the hard-neck garlic an inch or so (about 2.5 cm) above the bulb. As mentioned, you can also braid soft-neck garlic.

Store garlic cloves at 54°F to 59°F (12°C to 15°C), and they will keep for about six months.

SPRING ONIONS AND OTHER TYPES

There is something wonderful about crisp and fresh spring vegetables, and spring onions are among the very best of the season. These are simply onions harvested before they have fully developed.

The usual way to grow onions is from sets, also known as seed onions—small onions grown from seeds the year before, dug up, and dried before they are fully grown. Plant the seed onions in the ground in spring, and they will start to grow again and develop into full onion plants over the next few months.

Although using onion sets gives you a head start, it is also easy to start from seed. If you sow them in March, the onions will be ready for harvest in late July or early August, when the tops turn limp and lie flat on the ground. If you wait and let the tops wither, the onions will keep growing, but there is a risk of them cracking.

Once you harvest the onions, dry them, and leave the tops on. Either hang them in bunches in a well-ventilated place or lay them out on a mesh drying frame.

The Growing Process

A couple of years ago, I tried growing edible onions in containers for the first time. I planted the sets in April, at a depth of about 2 inches (5 cm) and about 4 inches (10 cm) apart. They soon sprouted and grew but began to bolt in the summer. Even though the flowers are really beautiful, it was unintended. Once they flower, onions are inedible.

It is well known that biennial vegetables like onions usually flower after winter. But sometimes they get a head start and flower in the first season. As described above, this may be due to a cold spell or perhaps a lack of water. But neither was the case, so I looked into it and found that the downside of onion sets is that they can bolt in the first season. This is less of a problem when sowing seecs.

This year, I opted for seeds. One of the benefits is the early harvest of spring onions. I sowed the seeds in trays with individual cells, planting four to f ve seeds in each. When the sprouts were about 2 inches (5 cm) tall, I transplanted them into pots, about 4 inches (10 cm) apart. After about eight weeks, the plants were big enough for me to harvest spring onions. I left the strongest plant in each group and pulled up the surrounding ones. It's a matter of quality over quantity.

CHARD

With its brightly colored stems in shades of yellow, red, orange, and pink, Swiss chard really brightens up the kitchen garden. In all honesty, I grow chard mainly for its decorative value. It's no great shakes in the kitchen. While the plants are still young, the leaves look beautiful in a salad bowl. When they are fully grown, you cook the colored stems and leaves separately. You can use the leaves like spinach, for example, in a stir-fry or stew.

The stems have several uses. They can be steamed, pickled, sautéed, or stir-fried in a wok with other vegetables. They add color to dishes with their bright hues, which fade somewhat when heated.

There is also a white variety known as silver beet. My grandma grew it in her kitchen garden and harvested it before the leaves grew too big and coarse. She served it creamed, which involved chopping the green parts and slicing the white, then adding grated nutmeg to bring out the flavor.

The Growing Process

Chard is quite easy to grow. It's an undemanding plant that doesn't require much in the way of nutrients. Seeds are available in both single varieties and mixed colors. You can sow them in a pot, and they will sprout soon afterwards. Even when the plants are very young, you can see what color the stems will be. They grow quickly, so it's a good idea not to wait too long before you harvest, because Swiss chard—especially when sown in early spring—often bolts and flowers. When sowing in late June or early July, that isn't as much of a problem. If you do that, you can enjoy the beautifully colored stems in late summer, not only in your container garden but also along with colorful flowers like dahlias, marigolds, and nasturtiums.

FENNEL

There are two types of fennel: bulb and leaf. Both taste like aniseed or licorice. It's a highly distinctive flavor that not everybody cares for, but I really like it.

The fennel that you find in supermarkets is bulb fennel. As the name suggests, it forms a bulb (which actually consists of swollen leaf sheaths), and it is usually sold without the feathery green leaves, which are also edible. With leaf fennel, only the leaves and seeds are used in cooking—the stems are often a bit woody. However, you can use them if harvested early, before the shoots grow taller than about 4 inches (10 cm). Harvesting at this stage doesn't harm the plant, which will soon sprout again.

Bulb fennel is an annual, while leaf fennel is a perennial. Bronze fennel, with its delicate golden foliage, is a particularly beautiful variety of leaf fennel.

The Growing Process

I must admit that I have found growing bulb fennel a bit of a challenge. The plants grow well, shoot up, and burst out into beautiful foliage but simply refuse to form the bulb, which is the whole point. I've tried several times: sowing early, sowing late, and making sure the plants have enough water. As we know, lack of water can stress plants.

But I'm not giving up. One tip I've read is that bulb fennel doesn't like its roots being disturbed when you transplant it. That makes sense, as you can't transplant root vegetables either. Next year, I'm going to sow in a tray with separate cells. I hope it works. But even if it doesn't, it won't be a complete disaster, as the green leaves are delicious.

Leaf fennel is much easier. It comes back faithfully year after year. I pick it regularly, especially in the spring. Towards the summer, I do it less often because I want the plants to flower. The beautiful yellow umbels, reminiscent of dill, are so pretty in bouquets.

Once the plants have flowered, seeds appear, and you can make a delicious spice with them. Harvest them when the color starts to change from green to brown. Spread out the seeds on a tray or plate, and leave them for a few weeks until they are dry enough to store. Fennel seeds are great in carrot and pumpkin soup, for example, as well as in bread. Some people also use them to flavor schnapps.

It is also worth mentioning that you don't need to use a lot of fertilizer with leaf fennel. Bulb fennel needs more, but only a little.

CORN

Corn is a beautiful, decorative plant that grows well in pots. It takes about three months from sowing to harvest. When the thread-like silks begin to wither, the cobs are ripe. You can also try loosening the husks that cover the kernels to see if they are golden and juicy.

When growing corn, it's important to get the timing right. If you harvest too early, the kernels have no flavor. Wait too long, and the sugar in the kernels turns to starch.

The Growing Process

Corn needs a lot of heat to thrive. For that reason, I don't sow in the greenhouse until around May 1. If you're sowing them outdoors, wait even a few more weeks.
I sow the seeds in individual pots, as the roots don't like to be disturbed. You can also sow seed in a larger pot, about 8 inches (20 cm) apart. In fact, it's good to sow two seeds at a time; if both sprout, you can remove the smaller plant without disturbing the other's roots. Using pruning shears is easiest.

When growing corn, it is advantageous to plant in clusters. If you plant them in rows in your kitchen garden, pollination might be a problem. Corn relies on the wind to blow pollen from the male flowers at the top of the plants to the female flowers below (the silks). If you grow it in rows, the pollen can just blow away.

As the plants grow, side shoots usually appear at the base. Remove them. After that, it's just a matter of enjoying the beautiful plants.

LEEKS

It's fairly easy to grow leeks in pots, especially if you buy a tray of seedlings from a garden center or nursery. It's not difficult to sow them, either. More on that below.

You can't help but be impressed by how quickly leeks grow once they get going.

They're a little slow at first, but when they suddenly take off, they grow really fast. The grayish-green foliage makes leeks highly decorative, and sometimes I leave them to overwinter in pots. I do this partly because they look beautiful alongside cabbage and partly because the following summer, leeks produce the most beautiful flowers, with large, globe-like heads. Later, you can harvest the seeds.

The Growing Process

It is important to note that there are both summer and winter leeks. Summer leeks are long and thin and must be picked before the frost arrives. Winter leeks, which are shorter and thicker, are fascinatingly resilient and can withstand subzero temperatures.

I sow summer leeks in trays in mid-March and winter leeks a month later. It's important not to sow them too close together. Instead, give them room to develop. An inch or so (about 2.5 cm) apart is optimal. Thin them out when the first young plants sprout.

In mid-May, transplant the leeks into pots with nutrient-enriched soil. Leave roughly 4 inches (10 cm) between the plants.

The white part of the leek is the most delicious. To maximize the long, pale stalks, you need to hill the earth around summer leeks as they grow. Partially fill the pot with soil, up to about 8 inches (20 cm) from the top edge. As the plants shoot up, add more soil.

Although the tender part of the leek is the most flavorsome, don't discard the green top. People often throw it out because it can contain quite a bit of sand and soil, but that's rarely the case when they are grown in pots.

CELERY

As you may know, there are two types of celery—leaf celery and the root vegetable known as celeriac. Here, I am talking exclusively about leaf celery, as celeriac grows so slowly that I don't find it suitable for growing in pots. Leaf celery, on the other hand, is perfect for containers.

You might have heard of "blanched celery," which simply refers to leaf celery that has been blanched by blocking sunlight, either by covering it with straw or hilling soil around it. Blanched celery is said to be slightly crisper and a little less bitter than regular celery, and its delicate green color looks beautiful in a salad, where it contrasts with darker tones.

One decorative variety is the red-stemmed 'Giant Red', which differs only in color, not in taste.

I really enjoy using celery in the kitchen, not only because of its flavor but also because of its crunchiness. I mainly use it in salads but sometimes in stir-fries and tomato sauce too. To preserve the crunchiness in hot dishes, I add the chopped celery at the very end.

The Growing Process

Celery seeds are tiny and need light to germinate. Press them lightly into moist potting soil, and don't cover them.

Sow in early March. When the plants are ready to be handled, transplant them to nutrient-enriched potting soil in trays with individual cells. Then leave them there to grow before moving them to pots and spacing them 8 to 10 inches (20 to 25 cm) apart.

Celery loves warmth, so don't move them outdoors until May. Harvest the celery in September, as even the slightest frost will ruin it.

Squash comes in many shapes and colors. They all taste pretty much the same, but I grow several different types just for the variety they add to my garden. One particularly attractive variety is 'Gray Zucchini', that is plump, round, and has green speckled skin.

SQUASH

If you've ever grown squash, you'll know that just one plant is enough to feed a family. I have several just because they come in so many interesting shapes, and I enjoy sharing them with my friends and colleagues. Most types of squash are green, but some are yellow. I especially like the yellow ones because they look so pretty alongside other vegetables in the garden and in salads.

The big yellow flowers are edible too. A few years ago, in Italy, I was served stuffed, deep-fried squash blossoms. They were delicious. The idea was new to me at the time, but I now sometimes see squash blossoms on sale in the summer months.

Squash plants produce both male and female blossoms, which are fairly easy to tell apart. Look closely at the female flowers, and you'll see a small squash beginning to grow at its base. The male flowers just hang from a green stem—these are the ones that are so delicious when deep-fried. However, it is also important to leave a few males for pollination.

You can cook squash in many different ways. Try barbecuing long slices, which will sear them with grill marks. Stir-fry them with other vegetables in a wok, or bake them in the oven, sprinkled with Parmesan. I often use squash to make soup and make large batches to freeze for later use. I do the same with many of my other summer vegetables. It's nice to have a ready supply of soup.

I especially enjoy growing 'Gold Rush' because its yellow color brightens up a salad bowl.

The growing process

To give my squash a head start, I plant them in the greenhouse and wait patiently until May. Squash loves heat and doesn't grow as quickly when it's cold. Start by planting the seeds in individual pots. After they sprout and have three to four leaves, transfer the plants to pots with a diameter of at least 14 to 16 inches (35 to 40 cm). Keep in mind that squash plants are large and lush. In addition to space, they need nutrition, so fertilizer is essential. Move the pots outdoors in mid-June.

If you don't have a greenhouse, sow the seeds outdoors after the danger of frost has passed. Garden-ready plants are another option. Buy them from nurseries and garden centers when they are in season.

BEANS

Although I have had a proper container kitchen garden for only the last couple of seasons, I've been growing beans for years because they are so beautiful and lush. Not only do they produce lovely flowers, but the beans are also decorative in their own right. As well as green beans, you will find purple, creamy yellow, and marbled varieties. Purple beans are particularly decorative but turn green when boiled.

The best-known beans are pole beans, which are climbers and reach a height of several feet (1 to 2 m). Plant them next to a trellis, arbor, or similar support structure. I grow pole beans on cone-shaped trellises in half wine barrels. This lets them reach a nice height. A suitable distance between pole bean plants is about 4 inches (10 cm).

Bush beans only grow to just over 1½ feet (45 cm). They grow particularly well in smaller pots with a diameter of 10 to 12 inches (25 to 30 cm), with five to seven plants in each. I stick branches into the soil between them to support the plants.

There are many types of beans with all sorts of different names in different countries, including French beans (*haricots verts*), Romano beans, runner beans, and dry beans.

French beans have small, round, thin pods. If the pods are big and flat, they may be Romano beans, while runner beans are decorative varieties with big, flat pods that are cut into smaller pieces before cooking. Bean types that are grown for their mature beans are known as dried beans.

Opposite: Many beans produce beautiful flowers, such as the orange blooms of the runner bean 'Scarlet Emperor'. They look extremely pretty in a salad.

Top: There are several varieties of bush beans in varying colors. This is 'Speedy', a green variety with an incredibly high yield.

Bottom: 'Purple Teepee' produces very dark beans. Unfortunately, they turn green when heated.

Beans contain lectins, which are toxins that can irritate the stomach. You need to steam or boil dried and fresh beans to render the lectins harmless. Boil fresh beans for only a few minutes so they retain their crispness.

Fresh beans are fantastic in hot and cold dishes. I always steam or boil a large portion so I have them ready for salads and other dishes. Beans are great in a potato salad with new potatoes—not only are they delicious, but they also add a beautiful splash of color.

When we grow beans in temperate climates, we usually intend to eat them fresh, and we harvest them before they are ripe, while they are still tender and delicate. If you leave them on the plant, the pods become coarse, and you can dry the beans. I'm not sure it's worth the effort, though, as dried beans are readily available and cheap.

The Growing Process

Beans are easy to grow as long as you remember that they need warmth (although fava beans are an exception to this rule). If you are growing them outdoors, don't sow until the soil is around 59°F (15°C), which is rarely the case before early June where I live.

I sow in the greenhouse around May 1 and would caution against starting much earlier. I speak from experience! If you're too impatient, the plants will grow too long and become entangled with each other, and it isn't easy to separate them again.

You can sow in seed trays or in pots.

When pole beans reach about 5 feet (1.5 m), it's a good idea to pinch off the top shoots to encourage the plants to form side shoots, which will produce more beans. Bush beans should be pinched off when they are 8 to 10 inches (20 to 25 cm) tall.

Opposite Top Left: Borlotti bean

Opposite Top Right: String bean 'Berggold'

Opposite Bottom Left: Pole bean 'Marvel of Venice'

Opposite Bottom Right: Runner bean 'Blauhilde'

BORLOTTI BEANS

Borlotti beans (sometimes called cranberry beans) are easy to recognize because they have decorative red-marbled pods. The beans themselves are white with red speckles. People usually let borlotti beans grow and eat the fresh beans, but you can eat them along with their pods, like snap beans, before they ripen. At this stage, they are greener.

FAVA BEANS

Fava beans, also known as broad beans, behave somewhat differently from pole beans and bush beans. First of all, they don't need as much heat. In fact, they can even withstand some frost. This means you can sow them in March. Sometimes, I sow a batch of seeds in late summer and overwinter them in the greenhouse, not only to harvest early but also because fava beans sown in late summer flower in May. At that stage, they look beautiful alongside flowers like tulips, especially the variety 'Crimson Flowered', which has reddish-purple blooms (see the picture on opposite page). The common varieties have white flowers with large dark spots.

Another advantage of 'Crimson Flowered' is that it only grows to a height of about 3 feet (1 m), whereas common fava beans reach a height of about 5 feet (1.5 m). The tall ones need support; 'Crimson Flowered' does not. The stems are stiff and upright, with beautiful gray-green leaves. Keep your plants about 6 inches (15 cm) apart.

Harvest the fava beans when the pods begin to swell and you can feel large beans inside. Pick the pods and blanche for a few minutes, then remove the beans.

Top: Before the seeds develop, borlotti beans can be eaten like snap beans. At this stage, they are a greenish color.

Bottom: When borlotti beans are ready to be picked, the pods are red and white.

Opposite Top Right: I grow the 'Crimson Flowered' variety because it has such beautiful flowers.

BERRIES

Like fruit trees, berry bushes have enjoyed a renaissance as kitchen gardens have gained popularity. In the past, berries were a staple of well-stocked kitchen gardens. I remember my grandma growing several of the most common types, including raspberries, red currants, black currants, and gooseberries. She made jam, used them in oatmeal, and froze some. At a time when people always served two courses for dinner, berries were indispensable.

One of my favorite summer desserts is a Danish specialty—red fruit jelly with cream. Mix equal parts raspberries, red currants, and quartered strawberries with cane sugar, about a quarter of the total weight of berries. Boil with real vanilla and juice from raspberries, red currants, and/or cherries, and then thicken with cornstarch. Season to taste with lemon juice and extra sugar. For an extra-special touch, stir in fresh berries before serving. This makes the dish even more delicious—a pure taste of heaven.

Another reason to grow berries is that they are extremely healthy. Some are even described as superfoods. Berries contain vitamins, minerals, antioxidants, micronutrients, and dietary fiber. The reason they are so good for us is mainly due to their small size. Most of the healthy substances in fruit are found in the skin, which in berries amounts to a much larger proportion of the total weight than in larger fruits.

The Growing Process

It's quite easy to grow berries. Pollination isn't usually a problem, because many berries are self-pollinating. On the other hand, it is sometimes advantageous to grow two different varieties, especially in the case of blueberries (see page 174).

Obviously, bees are also needed for pollination. Fortunately, berry flowers offer both nectar and pollen, so bees love them!

Plant them in pots with a diameter of about 12 inches (30 cm). I use nutrient-enriched potting soil and, of course, make sure to keep them well watered throughout the summer. Otherwise, there's not much to do but enjoy the buds, then the flowers, and finally the berries.

In early spring, before the bushes turn green, I repot them in fresh soil so that they're ready for a new season.

STRAWBERRIES

Strawberries are an ideal fruit for growing in pots. If you plant different varieties with varying harvest times, you will have fresh strawberries for two or three months a year. The first ones generally ripen in mid-June, but you can get an even earlier crop by placing the pots in the greenhouse and then moving them outside once you've picked the first berries. Strawberries grown in the open air taste better than those grown under glass.

There are many different varieties of strawberries. Early varieties such as 'Honeoye' and 'Earliglo' are particularly good. Another well-known variety is 'Senga Sengana', which ripens a little later. It has been popular for a long time—in fact, I remember my grandma often singing its praises. She also grew the Dutch variety 'Polka', which is both high yielding and tasty.

Another variety worth noting if you want late strawberries is 'Ostara'. What makes this variety special is that it is ever-bearing, meaning it blooms again, so you can have strawberries well into the late summer.

Most people probably associate strawberries with desserts and cakes. But their tartness also works well in savory dishes. I often use them in salads. Not only do they taste good, but they also add vivid color.

Having said that, I must admit that the berries I grow at home rarely make it as far as the kitchen. I tend to eat them straight from the plant.

The Growing Process

Every spring, nurseries and garden centers offer a wide selection of strawberry varieties. The plants are usually sold in trays of four or six. When planted in pots, they soon grow tall and leafy. In the first year, they produce only a few flowers and not many berries. The reason for this is that they use most of their energy establishing themselves and growing strong roots.

The best time to plant strawberries is the late summer, but they are rarely on sale at that time of year. Fortunately, it is easy to grow your own plants from runner cuttings in July.

Propagation

Strawberries form long runners with baby plants at their ends. In a normal strawberry bed, with plenty of soil around the plants, the runners take root by themselves. In pots, they need a little help. Fill small pots with soil, water well, and make sure the base of the leaves on the runners is in contact with the soil. To do this, bend metal wire to form "hairpins" that hold down the stems.

It won't take long, just a couple of weeks, for the runners to take root. You can then cut the "umbilical cord." After a few more weeks, when the roots fill the pot, transfer the small new plants into larger pots with a diameter of 10 to 12 inches (25 to 30 cm) and add fertilizer. Three plants per pot is a good number. The plants will now establish themselves. Next spring, they will produce fresh foliage. Don't add fertilizer at this stage. Otherwise, they will simply use their energy to develop leaves rather than berries.

Enjoy the beautiful flowers all through the spring, until it's time to harvest your strawberries.

RASPBERRIES

Raspberries come in several different varieties that ripen at different times and have different colors. Summer raspberries, which produce berries in June and July, have been the most popular until now. But autumn raspberries—which should probably be called late-summer raspberries, as they ripen in August and September—are catching up fast.

Worms in raspberries are caused by attacks by the raspberry beetle larva, a broad, 1/8-inch (4 mm) long yellow-brown beetle with characteristic club-shaped antennae. The larva, which is whitish with a brown-black head and three pairs of legs, grows up to just under 1/2 inch (1 cm).

The adult raspberry beetle emerges in May when the first buds appear on wild raspberries. It gnaws into the bud from the side, partially destroying it. The beetles also eat young leaves.

After about a week and a half, the egg hatches and the larvae, which live on their own, begin to eat the young fruit flesh. Over time, the fruit base becomes their main food source. At the end of summer, the larva leaves the fruit and hides in the soil, among withered plant parts. It forms a cocoon, in which it pupates after a few weeks. The raspberry beetle overwinters in or on the soil as a fully grown insect.

During the flowering season, you can collect the beetles by holding a dish with a little sulfur water underneath and tapping the stems of the plants so that the beetles fall into it. For this to be effective, you have to repeat it daily.

Keeping these beetles at bay is hard work, as is collecting Japanese beetles that enjoy feasting on raspberries in other parts of the world, including much of the United States. But, as mentioned, one workaround is to plant autumn raspberries. As they ripen late, the beetles and worms don't attack them.

Top: This little raspberry bush is called Lowberry 'Little Sweet Sister'. It produces berries on its annual shoots.

Autumn raspberries are big and beautiful and make perfect decorations on cakes and desserts. Although the differences are subtle, they don't taste quite as good as the summer ones.

Pruning

You should prune both summer and autumn raspberries after you harvest them.

Summer raspberries produce berries on shoots that grew the previous year. When you buy a plant in the spring, it has fresh shoots that will produce berries only the following year. The following season, it will develop side shoots that will produce flowers and berries later on. After you harvest the berries, cut the shoots they grew on at ground level. Don't cut the fresh, green shoots that sprout from the base in the meantime, as they will produce berries the following year.

Autumn raspberries are a bit simpler. They grow berries on their annual shoots, which means you can harvest them in the first year. Prune the shoots after harvesting or at the latest in early March, when fresh green shoots begin to appear at ground level. These are the ones that will produce berries in the fall.

A fairly new variety that produces berries on the annual shoots is called Lowberry 'Little Sweet Sister'. This variety grows well in pots. It reaches a height of less than 20 inches (1/2 meter) (hence the name), and the berries ripen as early as July. 'Raspberry Shortcake' is another dwarf variety available in the United States.

After a few seasons, once your raspberry plants reach a certain size, divide them into several pieces before replanting in the spring and moving them to new pots or beds.

Top: Autumn raspberry 'Autumn Bliss'
Bottom: Autumn raspberry 'Fall Gold'

GOOSEBERRIES

The main reason I grow gooseberries is that I love them in oatmeal and jam, but they're also really useful in savory dishes. Try this chutney recipe, for example: boil gooseberries, onions, raisins, sugar, salt, pepper, and vinegar with various spices such as ground ginger and allspice. It tastes heavenly.

Gooseberries also make excellent jam. Like apples, unripe gooseberries contain so much pectin that you need to add only sugar to make them gel. Add the berries to a saucepan, and cover them with water. Bring the berries to a boil, and cook for about ten minutes, then strain the juice through a cloth. Add an equal amount of sugar to the liquid, and boil for another ten minutes. To test if the jam is thick enough, dip a teaspoon into it, and let it drip off. If the last drop remains on the spoon, the jam is ready. If not, keep boiling so more of the water evaporates.

I have a feeling that people don't grow gooseberries much these days. Danes would once commonly add them to oatmeal, pickle them, and preserve them. I understand they are not common in the United States, but more and more people are now planting them. I think people don't like picking them because of the thorns, a problem growers have addressed by breeding varieties with fewer of them, like 'Captivator,' 'Pixwell,' and 'Friend Red Thornless.'

There are many varieties with round or oval berries in colors like green, yellow, and red. The berries vary in sweetness and acidity, and they can be completely smooth or downy. Like black currants and red currants, you don't need to prune gooseberries, but it's a good idea to thin them out after a few years by cutting the oldest branches all the way back to the soil.

BLACKBERRIES

There are two kinds of blackberries—with and without thorns—and they both ripen in late summer. I have grown only the thornless varieties because they don't grow quite as wildly as regular ones, which makes them better suited to growing in pots. They're also a bit more delicate, so you might want to keep them somewhere sheltered for the winter, like a greenhouse.

Blackberries grow fairly long canes. The thorny ones can easily reach 13 to 16 feet (4 to 5 m) tall, while the thornless ones are a little shorter, around 7 feet (2 m). The photograph opposite shows them being supported by a fence.

Growers have been breeding particularly compact varieties in recent years, such as Lowberry 'Little Black Prince', which reaches a height of only 3 feet (1 m) and doesn't need support—it's the variety shown in the photo below. Another variety, 'Baby Cakes', has even shorter shoots, making it suitable for hanging baskets as well as pots.

Like summer raspberries, blackberries produce new shoots from the base each spring, but flowers and berries usually grow only in the second year. I do have one variety that blooms on the annual shoots. It is the Lowberry 'Little Black Prince', which I mentioned above.

Cut the shoots off at the base after you pick the berries.

BLACK CURRANTS

Black currants are quite tart, so I don't eat them straight from the bush. Blackbirds do, though, often before they're ripe.

I love black currant jam. Black currant juice is also a favorite. When I was a kid, it was synonymous with the brand Ribena. I thought this was a Danish product but later discovered it is British, and the name was inspired by the Latin for black currant, *Ribes nigrum*.

The first bottles of Ribena saw the light of day in Bristol in 1938. The high vitamin C content encouraged hospitals to buy it during World War II for use as a dietary supplement. Ribena has been available in Denmark since 1948.

Another well-known black currant product is crème de cassis, a heavenly tasting French liqueur. I have found a great-sounding recipe online. I haven't tried it yet, but it's only a matter of time! Once my black currants ripen, I'll be ready:

Take just over a quart (1 liter) of unflavored vodka, 24.6 ounces (700 g) of black currants, about 20 black currant leaves, and 21.1 ounces (600 g) of sugar. Mash the berries with a fork, and mix them with the sugar and chopped leaves. Pour the mixture into a large preserving jar or similar container, and pour the vodka over the top.

Leave the mixture in a dark place for ten to twelve weeks, but shake the jar daily. Just before the three-month mark, strain the black-currant mixture and bottle the liqueur. Don't throw out the black currant mixture—it can be used to add some intense flavor to desserts, such as ice cream, or as an accompaniment to pancakes.

The liqueur benefits from being left to stand in the bottle for a month. Add more sugar if you find it too sour.

The black currant bush has the most beautiful leaves, although the flowers are rather inconspicuous. They bloom quite early, in late April, and are so small that it's surprising that the bees can find them. But find them they do, thankfully, because without them there would be no berries at all.

I grow several varieties of black currants with varying ripening times. I am particularly fond of the tree variety 'Titania', partly because of the way the berries hang beautifully from the "crown."

Both black currants and gooseberries are also available as standard trees, which are grafted onto a rootstock of golden currant, *Ribes aureum*.

Pruning

Black currants bloom on second-year shoots. You don't need to prune the bushes to get berries. In fact, for the first three to four years, you can leave the shears in the shed. After that, it may be a good idea to start thinning out. Do this by cutting back the oldest branches right down to the ground every year or every second year. This will encourage new branches to grow, gradually rejuvenating the bush.

Similarly, don't prune standard trees for about three years. After that, cut the shoots that produced berries to about 4 inches (10 cm).

If you want to propagate black currants, it is best to do so by taking cuttings rather than dividing the plant. In early spring, cut off 8-inch (20 cm) woody shoots and plant them (see pages 288–289).

Another option is layering. Take a hook made of strong metal wire, attach it to a low-growing side branch, and secure it to the ground. It is important that at least one of the dormant buds makes contact with the soil, as it is from here that the roots will grow.

The bud is more likely to form roots if it not only touches the ground but is also covered by an inch (few centimeters) of soil that is kept moist at all times. The roots will appear within a few months. Once they have developed, sever the connecting branch and pot the new plant.

RED CURRANTS

When it comes to growing them, there's little difference between red currants and black currants. The beautiful red berries look very tempting, especially to the birds, who will swoop in at the first flash of crimson. Blackbirds are particularly fond of them. We have quite a few blackbirds in the garden, and I'm very grateful for them. Although I often have to share my harvest with them, I couldn't imagine the garden without birds in general—blackbirds in particular.

This year, I will try a variety with white berries, 'White Dutch' (see the next page). Maybe it won't attract as much attention.

I am sure that many people feel the same, but here in Denmark, the song of the blackbird is one of the surest signs of spring. When the males announce their presence in February, it heralds the start of a new gardening season.

In winter, blackbirds are frequent visitors to the bird feeder, where they and other garden birds feast on seeds and bread but also boiled potatoes, rice, and other kitchen scraps. Apples are a particular favorite.

Many of us have noticed that blackbirds almost seem tame, as they follow us around the garden when we start digging and cultivating. It's because our activity brings worms to the surface, and blackbirds are constantly on the hunt for them.

When a male blackbird wants to assert his territory and attract females, he finds a tree or other high place, perches on it, and sings. If other males come too close, he chases them away. Sometimes it ends in a fight. The male also has an alarm call, which he uses to warn other members of the species if birds of prey or other dangers lurk.

Female blackbirds build nests, while the males gather nesting materials, such as twigs, small sticks, dry grass, and leaves for lining. Garden hedges and bushes are their preferred locations, but blackbirds also sometimes find their way into human-built structures—in our case, the old horse stable behind the garage. One year, a female nested in the teeth of an upside-down pitchfork, so we couldn't use it that summer.

The female lays three to five blue-green eggs with brown spots, which hatch after just a couple of weeks. About fourteen days after hatching, the chicks are ready to fly the nest—literally. The blackbird pair are then ready to produce a new brood. They reuse the nest, and the female incubates two to three broods per season.

Enough bird talk. Back to the red currants . . .

If I get to the red currants before the birds, I like to put a few handfuls in a jar, add 2 to 3 tablespoons of cane sugar, replace the lid, and shake well. It tastes delicious as an accompaniment to chicken and other meat dishes. To me, this is the taste of summer, along with new potatoes and fresh cucumber salad.

Red currant jelly is another favorite. As my grandma used to say, red currant jelly is made "pound for pound"—you use equal weights of berries and sugar. To make the jelly set, you have to pick the berries before they are fully ripe, as that's when they contain the most pectin. A natural gelling agent, pectin is named after the Greek word *pektos*, which means "set" and "firm."

Other fruits and berries rich in pectin include unripe apples and gooseberries.

BLUEBERRIES

Blueberries grow well in pots and look beautiful all year round. In spring, the plants form white or pale-pink bell-shaped flowers. In summer, the berries change from green to waxy blue. In the fall, the foliage takes on the most impressive autumn colors, and in winter, the bare branches are a beautiful fiery red.

Blueberries are self-pollinating to a small extent, but it is a good idea to have at least two different varieties, as this will produce a better yield, with more and larger berries. It doesn't really matter which varieties you choose. It is just simpler with blueberries than with tree fruits, because with tree fruits, you need to have compatible types.

There are a number of different species. For example, the wild blueberry (*Vaccinium myrtillus*) is native to a band of northern regions spanning the globe that includes northern Europe, Asia, Canada, and the Pacific Northwest region of the United States. It is quite short, around 6 to 14 inches (15 to 35 cm). The bog bilberry (*Vaccinium uliginosum*) is another wild variety. The standard garden variety is usually the large-fruited American blueberry, *Vaccinium corymbosum*. A couple of extra-compact varieties are also available, 'Elliott' and 'Darrow', which grow to a height of around 3 feet (1 m), ideal for growing in pots. Dwarf varieties in the US include 'Jelly Bean', 'Top Hat', 'Sunshine Blue', and 'Mini Blues'.

Wild blueberries (*Vaccinium myrtillus*) are instantly recognizable by their dark, almost bluish flesh, which stains easily. In contrast, both American blueberries and bog bilberries have very light-colored flesh.

The Growing Process

It is important to note that blueberries are acidophilic plants, so you need to plant them in acidic soil. In containers, use a potting mix that contains sphagnum peat. It is better to water them with rainwater, as tap water may be alkaline depending on where you live.

Blueberries don't need a great deal of nutrients. A handful of rhododendron fertilizer or chicken manure pellets in early spring will do the trick.

Like black currants and raspberries, blueberries don't require special pruning, but after a few years, it's advisable to thin out the bushes by cutting away the oldest and thickest branches at the base.

FRUIT TREES

Growing fruit trees in pots is a wonderful experience, especially if you have children. Watching the different fruits blossom, develop, and ripen is absolutely enchanting. The trees also add some nice height as a contrast to other potted plants.

Garden centers and nurseries reported a significant increase in sales of fruit trees and berry bushes in recent years. More and more people want to grow edible crops so they know where their food comes from, and fruit trees are particularly easy to grow.

It comes as a surprise to a lot of people that you can grow fruit trees in pots. But you can—and it's not hard. Of course, the pot needs to be a certain size, and you have to remember to water and fertilize the tree, but that's no different from other plants. And it probably goes without saying that a tree needs more water than, for example, lettuce.

The size of the pot depends on the size of the tree. For a 3-foot (1 m)-tall fruit tree (a typical size for a short one from a garden center), a pot with a diameter of about 14 inches (35 cm) is suitable. As it grows, the tree will need to be repotted, usually every year or two. This should be done in early spring, before the leaves sprout. The first few times, transplant it into gradually bigger pots, preferably with an extra diameter of 6 to 8 inches (15 to 20 cm) each time. Obviously, you can't keep doing this forever, because eventually the pot would become impractically large. After repotting a few times, I recommend pruning the roots, replanting, and adding fresh soil.

Grafting

Fruit trees are grafted onto special rootstocks, which determine how tall the trees will grow. For growing in pots, it's important to choose rootstocks that will grow to a modest height. The rootstocks have different names, which are listed under the respective fruits.

Slow-growing rootstocks also have another advantage: the tree bears fruit at an early age. The tree doesn't need as much energy to grow, so it expends more energy producing fruit. As a rule, this means that you can harvest in the first year, which is worth knowing before you buy. If you graft yourself, it typically takes four to five seasons for apples and pears, and even longer for plums and cherries.

If you are confident enough to try grafting, rootstocks are easy to find online. You will also need grafting scions. You can either buy these or cut them from an apple or a pear tree.

Apples and pears are definitely the easiest to graft. Plums and cherries are slightly more difficult. Note, however, that not all pear varieties are equally simple. In fact, you might even need to double graft (see page 184).

If you are looking for a specific fruit variety, consult regional sources and agricultural universities for information on varieties that grow well where you live.

I myself have never grafted, but it is definitely something I would like to try. There are limits to how many fruit trees I can fit in my garden, but the process itself fascinates me. And there are always buyers for fruit trees.

There are many excellent instructional videos on YouTube and elsewhere, and you can even take courses in grafting.

'Red Pineapple', a German cultivar, is a delicious apple that grows to a modest height. Don't leave the apples on the tree for too long, or they will lose their crispness and delicate tart flavor.

Pollination

For fruit to grow, flowers need to be pollinated, a process that involves pollen being transferred from the anthers of one flower to the stigma of another. This can be done by the wind or by bees and other insects. Many fruit trees, such as apples and pears, need to be pollinated by other nearby trees. This is called "cross-pollination."

An apple tree must be pollinated by another apple tree, and the same applies to pears. However, not all varieties can pollinate each other. Pollination charts are available online that show which varieties are compatible, taking into account flowering time and other hereditary characteristics.

In a rural residential area with a lot of gardens, there is a good chance that a neighbor will have a matching fruit tree, but you can't count on that in every neighborhood. One solution is a "family" tree, that is, one onto which several different varieties have been grafted, each of which pollinate each other. Apples, pears, plums, and cherries are available as family trees grafted onto rootstocks that grow to a modest height. This solves the problem of pollination and means you can have several varieties in a limited space.

As an alternative method, I have also heard that you can cut flowering branches from suitable fruit trees (make sure you ask permission first!) and put them in a bucket of water close to the tree you want to pollinate.

Some plum and cherry varieties don't need help from another tree, as they are self-pollinating.

Pollinating insects are just as important as a suitable source of pollen. Wind alone is rarely enough.

Wasps, flies, and mosquitoes are all helpful, but bumblebees, honeybees, and several other wild bee species are the best pollinators, so it's important to attract them. You can do this by growing plants with a high pollen and nectar content, such as blackberries, blueberries, raspberries, red currants, and black currants. Herbs such as chives, marjoram, sage, and thyme are also good bee plants. The same applies to pea flowers, both the edible species and the beautiful lathyrus (sweet peas).

I grow a number of edible flowers, several of which attract bees. That way, I get both food and pollen. Marigolds, African marigolds, and nasturtiums are some of the bees' favorites. They also love sunflowers, which I grow in pots.

Bees

Bees live on nectar, which they collect from flowers. As they fly from flower to flower, they collect pollen, the male reproductive cells, which they take home to the larvae in their hive.

The honeybee may well be the one we know best, but there are thousands of other bee species around the globe.

Honeybees

Honeybees are said to be the most numerous domesticated creatures. They live in hives, with up to sixty thousand bees in a single colony. Each colony consists of a queen, several hundred drones (all male), and thousands of workers.

Manmade bee hives have vertical panels, on each side of which the workers build small hexagonal wax cells. Some of these cells store honey, while others contain eggs, larvae, and pupae. The bees cover the inside of the hive with a substance called propolis (also known as "bee glue"), which they make from beeswax mixed with saliva and plant resin.

A beekeeper can harvest 110 to 175 pounds (50 to 80 kg) of honey a year from a colony, but that's only about one-eighth of the honey produced. The bees and their larvae eat the rest.

Wild Bees

There are thousands of different species of wild bees, of which many are bumblebees. Throughout spring and summer, the small, furry, and heavily laden bumblebees fly from flower to flower to collect pollen and nectar. They collect nectar in their honey sac and pollen in the "pollen baskets" on their hind legs.

Many of the other species are known as solitary bees and don't produce honey.

Pruning

I am occasionally asked for advice on pruning shrubs and trees. I can speak confidently about shrubs, but I don't have much experience with trees in general or fruit trees in particular. Online searches often leave me more confused than when I started, but I did find a short and useful summary on the website of the National Association for Practical Ecology. I have been given permission to reproduce it here. Sten Porse from their expert panel writes,

Let's get one thing straight: pruning isn't necessary, but it can be practical. It doesn't make trees bear more fruit, but it does mean the tree's resources are focused on fewer, but larger fruits. It is for these two reasons—practicality and larger fruits—that various methods of pruning have been developed over time.

The basic principle is that the tree itself has genetic traits that control both branch growth and fructification. If we intervene, the tree responds to the best of its ability. If we prune skillfully enough, the tree's response will be exactly what we wanted.

Basic Rules for Pruning

Providing detailed pruning advice would require an entire book, but here are some basic rules:

- Prune as little as possible.
- Create the trunk and the permanent branch skeleton as early as possible in the tree's life—and don't touch them later.
- If you want a few but large fruits, stick to three or four main branches, removing the rest early on.
- Ensure that the tree always has enough leaves to produce the sugar needed for the fruit to grow, but also make sure that all of the fruit receives light.
- Cut any tall, vertical shoots above the fourth bud, so that they form four short shoots each. Don't remove the short ones.
- Don't use nitrogenous fertilizers (marked N on the declaration). Use phosphate in June and lime in August (if you live where the soil is naturally acidic).
- Prune in July–August, regardless of the type of fruit.

In colder parts of North America, it is often recommended to prune fruit trees in their dormant season of winter.

Spindle Trees

It is worth mentioning a special type of small tree that is ideal for growing in pots—spindle trees. These are trees with thin horizontal side branches, which grow in a spiral around a strong trunk. Once the trunk reaches the desired height of 6.5 to 8.2 feet (2 to 2.5 m), you can prune it into a pyramid/Christmas tree shape. I understand they are difficult to source in North America.

Columnar Trees

Columnar trees have become very popular with apple growers in recent years. They are ideal not only for growing in pots but also for small gardens, because they don't take up much space. They form quite short side shoots on their strong trunk, which you should cut back regularly to just 2 inches (5 cm).

You might also hear columnar trees referred to as "Brussels sprout trees." This is because when they bear fruit, they resemble sprouts on a stalk.

Fruit Thinning

Experienced fruit growers and gardeners sometimes talk about "June drop," which refers to the phenomenon of fruit trees shedding some of their fruit in late June or early July. They do this because fruit trees—especially apple, pear, and plum—often grow more fruit than the tree can bear, and the trees shed many of the smallest ones. But if you want your fruit to be of the highest quality, the June drop isn't always enough, and you have to further thin out the fruit. This both prevents the branches from breaking and allows light and air to reach the fruit that will be harvested in late summer. The remaining fruits should be the biggest and have no visible defects.

A tree has only limited energy, so if it grows excessive amounts of fruit, it can affect the following year's flower buds, meaning it will bear fruit only every other year.

When thinning fruit, a good rule of thumb is that there should be about a dozen leaves for each apple or pear. This applies to the whole tree. It is easy enough to follow the rule when trees are young, but it is a little more time consuming to count the leaves on a tree that is several years old. Fortunately, it's only a rough guide.

The rule of thumb for plums is that there should be about a hand's width between each one.

APPLES

Before I became really interested in gardening, I used to wonder why the apple trees in new gardens didn't have the same charming gnarled shape as those in my grandparents' garden.

One reason is that it takes a very long time for fruit trees to become gnarled and crooked. Another is that the rootstocks used for grafting in the old days were often wild strains. A third reason is that back then, some trees were grown from seeds (although I don't think my grandparents' trees were).

Growing apple trees from seed requires tremendous patience and is a bit of a gamble. It takes years before the first apples appear, and you can't predict how they will taste due to cross-pollination by bees flying from tree to tree. If you are very lucky, you might grow a completely new and tasty variety, which you can then propagate by grafting.

In many parts of the world, along ditch edges and railway embankments, you might see a number of wild apple trees, which have most likely grown because passersby have thrown away apple cores over the years. If you pick an apple from one of them and taste it, the likelihood is that it will be extremely sour. Finding a good new apple variety is a bit like finding a needle in a haystack.

As mentioned, the rootstock determines the height of the tree. The rootstocks have different number and letter designations. The most common dwarfing rootstock for apples is M9, which is slow growing and therefore particularly suitable for pots. The same applies to M26, which grows a little larger but still only moderately.

The most suitable varieties are those that already have a slow growth rate. Some of my favorites are 'Discovery', 'James Grieve', 'Guldborg', 'Red Pineapple', and 'Red Aroma'.

PEARS

Apples and pears are often mentioned in the same breath. But pears are less common, mainly because pear trees are not quite as hardy as apple trees. The flowers bloom early in the spring, which makes them more vulnerable to frost. If there are no flowers, there will be no fruit. The advantage of planting a pear in a pot is that you can move it to a warmer spot during cold periods.

Low- to medium-growth pears are grafted onto quince rootstocks, usually quince A, which grow to a moderate size.

Grafting pears can be challenging, because some varieties find it difficult to grow into the quince rootstock, while others don't. The latter group, which are known as *compatible* varieties, includes 'Bonne Louise', 'Clara Frijs', and 'Pierre Corneille'.

Conversely, 'Clapp's Favorite', 'Grev Moltke', 'Charneu', and 'Williams' are problematic and classified as *incompatible*. These varieties have to be double-grafted. This means that the scion is joined with an intermediate variety—often 'Clara Frijs'—and then this fusion is grafted onto the quince.

With its sweet and aromatic taste, 'Clara Frijs' is an unrivaled pear. I harvest it before it is fully ripe, which makes it extra crisp.

PLUMS

Few fruits are more delicious than sun-ripened, sweet, juicy plums. They are quite different from the large, round, hard, red-and-blue imported plums available year-round, which I don't think are worth eating.

After conducting research into fruit trees, I have chosen 'Opal', which I've heard described as "probably the best plum tree for the garden."

St. Julien A, a moderate-growth rootstock, is often used for grafting p ums. Wavit is another rootstock recommendation.

There is nothing quite as delicious as a fully ripe 'Opal' plum, a variety that is also recommended by professional gardeners.

SWEET CHERRIES

There are two main types of cherry: sweet and sour. Contrary to what you might think, the distinction isn't just about taste. The difference is that sweet cherries are edible, while sour ones are used to make juice, wine, cherry sauce, and desserts.

Most people, including myself, would probably choose a sweet cherry that you can nibble on, if the birds don't get there first. Birds—especially starlings and blackbirds—are just as fond of cherries as humans. I know from experience that this can be a big problem! In my first season as a cherry grower, a couple of blackbirds made a big dent in my crop. I covered the tree with a net, but a little too late. Still, I did manage to claim a few for myself.

The variety I grow is 'Stella', which is self-pollinating and has beautiful, delicious, deep-red fruit. There are also yellow cherries, a well-known variety being 'Rainier'. The fruit grower—and my good friend—Erling Nielsen strongly recommends yellow varieties, precisely because they don't attract birds.

Low-growth cherry trees are grafted onto the Gisela 5 rootstock, which produces a tree with a final height of approximately 6 to 7 feet (2 m).

'Stella' is a popular cherry variety with large, tasty berries. One advantage is that it is self-pollinating.

FIGS

Although our winters have become milder, it can still be difficult to grow figs outdoors in more northerly regions. Fortunately, they thrive in pots, which can be moved into a greenhouse or garage during winter.

In temperate places, you can see impressive fig trees that are up to 13 feet (3 or 4 m) tall and just as wide. In a pot, they don't grow taller than 6 or 7 feet (around 2 m).

In the Mediterranean region, fig trees bear fruit up to three times a year. That doesn't happen in more northerly latitudes. In milder winters, the walnut-sized fruits can overwinter outdoors. They ripen in late summer.

It is worth growing figs for their foliage alone, as the leaves are highly distinctive and exceptionally beautiful. They can also be used in the kitchen. For example, fresh fig leaves can be used to flavor oil or ice cream or to wrap fish before cooking.

I also enjoy the sight of fig trees in the fall, when the leaves develop the most beautiful golden hue.

The Growing Process

Apart from their sensitivity to frost, figs are not difficult to grow in pots. Use fertilizer sparingly, because if you give them too much nutrition, they will use the energy to produce leaves instead of fruit.

Fruit set also improves if the bush/tree is "stressed" a little—in other words, fig plants thrive when they are a bit cramped, so don't repot them too often.

Propagation from Cuttings

If you know a gardener with a lush and productive fig bush or tree with lots of fruit, they may be generous enough to give you a cutting. Figs are quite easy to propagate. The best time to do so is in March or April: stick a 6- to 8-inch (15 to 20 cm)-long shoot into moist seed-starting potting soil, and cover with a plastic bag (see pages 288–289). It can take up to two months for the woody shoot to take root. Once the roots are visible through the holes in the bottom of the pot, it is time to repot in nutrient-enriched potting soil.

JERUSALEM ARTICHOKES

Few vegetables are as easy to grow as Jerusalem artichokes. So much so that they can be quite rampant. Just a single tuber left in the ground sends out runners and soon turns into many more. Before you know it, the tall, green plants have taken over several square feet (meters). That's why it makes perfect sense to grow Jerusalem artichokes in pots, because it keeps them under control.

The Growing Process

While Jerusalem artichokes are easy to grow, they do require ample nutrients if you want them to be large and vigorous. Plant the tubers just as you would for potatoes, except there's no need to presprout.

When growing potatoes, you usually buy special seed potatoes to avoid disease. However, I have never come across "seed Jerusalem artichokes" and don't know if they even exist. I buy large, attractive, organic tubers instead. Always choose organic, as it means they haven't been sprayed with a sprout inhibitor.

Plant the tubers in April or May. They will be ready for harvest in fall, once the foliage begins to wither. You don't have to harvest them all at once, as the tubers are not vulnerable to frost and will remain fresh in the ground.

Take a pot that is about 12 inches (30 cm) high, with a diameter of about 14 inches (35 cm), and fill it two-thirds full of soil. Place three or four tubers on the top, fill the pot with soil, and water well. Within a few weeks, green shoots will appear above the surface. Over the course of the season, they will grow tall and sturdy.

The tall green shoots on the left are from Jerusalem artichokes.

BEETS

The days when we enjoyed beets only pickled are long gone. Now, we grate them and eat them raw in salads, bake or roast them in the oven, pan-fry them, and press them to make juice. The possibilities are endless.

There are many varieties of beet—thick and thin, round and long—and not all of them are red. White, yellow, and candy-striped types brighten up the scene. I grow all the colors, but mostly reds, because that's what I use most in the kitchen. The yellow and white beets have a slightly milder flavor than the red ones. You can bake them in the oven with other vegetables since they don't change the color of the other ingredients. Neither do 'Chioggia' beets, but when heated, their stripes disappear. You can prevent that by serving them raw. I slice them very thinly, marinate the slices, and use them in salads.

The Growing Process

It takes about four months from sowing to harvesting beets, so if you start in the greenhouse in late winter, the beets will be ready around mid-summer. The seeds are sown in pots. To avoid unnecessary thinning, space them about 2½ to 3½ inches (6 to 9 cm) apart in the soil, which is relatively easy because the seeds are quite large. Older varieties are known as cluster seeds or multigerm seeds. These composite seeds can produce up to three or four sprouts. Seeds from cultivars that produce only one seedling per seed are easy to come by. When the plants have grown a little, thin them out and keep them 2 to 3 inches (5 to 8 cm) apart. Harvest the beets before they fill the pot, that is, when they are 2½ to 2¾ inches (6 to 7 cm) in diameter. Larger ones tend to be too coarse.

Top: The 'Bull's Blood' variety has deep-red leaves.
Bottom: The inside of a 'Chioggia' beet is truly enchanting.
Opposite top: 'Moulin Rouge'
Opposite bottom: 'Burpee's Golden'

BRASSICAS

I love brassicas (members of the cabbage family)! Not just in the garden but in the kitchen too. And I'm definitely not the only one. At least not when it comes to cooking with them. In recent years, brassicas have become cool, and for good reason. They are filling, superhealthy, and you can cook them in all sorts of ways.

There are so many beautiful and decorative species and varieties of the cabbage family that are ideal for growing in pots in summer, fall, and even winter. Several members of the cabbage family are extremely hardy and resistant to frost—kale, for example. The fact that it produces the most beautiful light-yellow flowers in spring is an added bonus.

Brassicas are quite easy to grow, as long as you tackle one big problem—caterpillars. In early summer, white cabbage butterflies begin to become active, and it's quite likely that they'll find your crops and lay eggs. After a few days, the eggs hatch and caterpillars appear. You really need to watch out for them. They can devour an entire plant in no time.

One effective defense against cabbage butterflies is to cover the plants with row cover or insect netting, but it's not very attractive. Another option is to hunt for eggs a couple of times a week. There are a few different types of cabbage butterfly, and they lay eggs in different ways. Some cabbage butterfly species lays eggs individually on the underside of leaves, while others lay them in groups of about fifty. If you don't get rid of them all, larvae will soon appear, and you'll have to hunt them down.

Another way to combat them is to spray the leaves with a nontoxic bacterial preparation, *Bacillus thuringiensis*. The product, often called Bt, is used by organic farmers. When the caterpillars eat the leaves, they stop eating and die within a few days. Respray about once a week.

The Growing Process

Pests aside, growing brassicas isn't hard. The seeds don't take long to germinate, and you can extend the harvest season over a whole year if you choose different types. Some are suitable for summer growing, while others are perfect for winter.

The cabbage family is extremely broad. Some species are particularly suitable for early sowing and harvesting. Others are easier and better later in the season, such as broccoli, cauliflower, and Asian leafy vegetables.

In March, I sow kohlrabi, pointed cabbage, and savoy cabbage, which are ready to harvest in the summer. I also sow Brussels sprouts, kale, and Tuscan kale at this time, mainly because of their decorative value in summer.

At the end of June, I sow kohlrabi, pointed cabbage, Savoy cabbage, kale, Tuscan kale, broccoli, and cauliflower. They grow a little slower than those sown in the spring but are beautiful in the fall and winter. Make sure that you harvest pointed cabbage and Savoy cabbage before the weather turns too cold.

In June, I also sow Asian varieties, such as bok choy, komatsuna, and mizuna.

As the picture on the right shows, I grow a lot of brassica plants—in fact, far too many for my container garden. I plant the surplus in the garden beds as an accompaniment to perennials and summer flowers. They look beautiful throughout the summer, and they embellish the garden during fall and winter. They are perhaps at their most attractive the following spring, when they bolt and start to flower.

TURNIPS

It may not be immediately apparent from their name, but botanically speaking, turnips are part of the *Brassica* family.

I grow the 'Purple Top' variety, mainly because it's so decorative. Before I started growing turnips, I had never cooked them. I would pass them by on supermarket shelves because I didn't have a clue what to do with them. But now I do.

Turnip is a fairly versatile vegetable with a slightly sweet flavor. You can eat it raw, baked, or fried. If you serve it raw, make sure to slice it very thinly.

The Growing Process

Turnips are a fascinating vegetable that develops quite quickly. If you sow them in March, they will be ready for harvest in late May. Make sure you harvest them on time. Turnips are at their most delicious when slightly bigger than ping-pong balls. If you wait too long, they will flower.

Even though you can harvest in May, it makes sense to wait until late July to sow turnips and then harvest them in early fall. Sowing later means they won't bolt as quickly, and you can wait until they are the size of a clenched fist before harvesting them. Just don't leave them too late, because turnips can't tolerate frost.

KOHLRABI

Kohlrabi is one of the most unusual and decorative members of the cabbage family. It comes in both green and purple varieties, and really stands out in a container kitchen garden.

I'm sure a lot of readers will have seen kohlrabi in their local supermarket and wondered how to use it. I became curious about it while writing green cookbooks. I soon discovered that it's not only delicious, but highly versatile. You can grate, chop, or finely slice it and put it in salads. You can bake, fry, and even pickle it. If I had to describe the flavor, I would say it is like a milder version of a broccoli stalk.

The plant develops a round stem node an inch or so (a couple of centimeters) above the ground, to which the leaves are attached. As it grows, it loses some of the leaves, leaving a scar.

I sow twice per season—in the greenhouse in March and outside in late June. I harvest around midsummer, when the kohlrabi are the size of tennis balls and super-delicious. This also means I don't have to worry about caterpillars, because, here, the first cabbage butterflies don't usually arrive until early July.

The second batch will be ready in late summer or fall. They grow somewhat slower than the first batch, but I also like to let them grow a bit more. And while they're not quite as delicate as the first batch, they're still good, especially in winter, when the season calls for more robust vegetables. Another good thing about kohlrabi is that it is relatively resistant to frost and can tolerate temperatures down to around 14°F (–10°C).

If you let kohlrabi overwinter, it will produce beautiful light-yellow flowers. As with other flowers in the cabbage family, they taste really good.

Bottom: 'Delikatesse Witte' is one of the many kohlrabi varieties.
Opposite: 'Azurstar' grows quite quickly.

Top: 'Cuor di Bue Grosso' is a particularly early pointed cabbage with a smaller head.

Opposite: 'Vysoke' is the name of this fine purple pointed cabbage.

POINTED CABBAGE

Pointed cabbage is one of my favorite summer ingredients. Finely chopped, it's indispensable both as a raw vegetable and in a regular green salad, either instead of or as a supplement to regular lettuce. Occasionally, I also stew it or use it in wok dishes. Perhaps best of all, grilled or baked halves or quarters are a real delicacy, especially when garnished with butter, breadcrumbs, and Parmesan. It's really worth growing this delicious crop.

Most people are familiar with green pointed cabbage, but the purple variety is becoming increasingly common, which is a welcome development, because it is particularly decorative. As an added bonus, it mostly keeps its beautiful color when cooked, unlike purple beans, for example, which turn green as soon as you heat them.

Even when the plants are relatively small, you can see the inner leaves beginning to form a point. Every day, the shape becomes a little bit more apparent. I harvest the first pointed cabbages in early July—just in time to serve them with fresh peas and new potatoes. The perfect summer food!

SAVOY CABBAGE

With its wrinkled surface and almost leathery leaves, this is a unique and strikingly beautiful cabbage. It tastes best cooked, for example, finely chopped and stir-fried in a wok or frying pan. It is also used to make cabbage rolls—minced meat wrapped in a cabbage leaf and fried in butter in a pan. My grandma often made these for family gatherings. She used white cabbage leaves and called them white cabbage roulettes. They are a fond childhood memory.

CAULIFLOWER

Not much compares to a freshly harvested head of cauliflower. But it's important not to overcook it. Lots of us distinctly remember the taste and smell of overcooked cauliflower from our childhood and have no wish to go back there. But cooked well, whether boiled, fried, or baked—and even raw—cauliflower is incredibly delicious. It is important to retain the crispness. If the cauliflower is finely chopped and served raw with a good oil and vinegar dressing, it tastes quite nutty. The leaves are delicious too.

Growing cauliflower has been a bit of a challenge for me, because the first batch I sowed in March started to flower before the heads had developed. In fact, a cauliflower head is a collection of tightly packed flower buds. I don't know if the unwanted flowering was due to temperature fluctuations or whether the plants dried out at some point. I had better luck with the second sowing in late June and harvested fine little heads in early October.

Bottom: 'Aubervilliers' is a well-known and highly recommended variety of Savoy cabbage.

Opposite Bottom: I grow several different varieties of cauliflower. This is 'Snowball'. In the picture at the bottom right, you can see how I break the green leaves and fold them over the head to encourage further blanching. This doesn't add any culinary value—it is purely cosmetic.

When harvesting broccoli, I leave some of the stalk behind. This allows the plant to shoot again if it's not too late in the season. This variety is called 'Rasmus'.

BROCCOLI

Like cauliflower, broccoli is a "flower vegetable." In other words, it consists of a bouquet of undeveloped flower buds. Broccoli is also a little tricky to grow. It tends to flower quickly in the summer, although I have harvested beautiful heads in late summer, as well as smaller bouquets.

If your broccoli starts to flower, don't despair. The flowers are beautiful. They are also edible, as are the stems and leaves. If you cut off the flowering head, small mini broccoli will often sprout from the junctures of the leaves. The same happens when you harvest a nonflowering head.

BOK CHOY

Beautifully plump with a narrow waist, few vegetables are as well-formed and elegant as bok choy, an Asian cabbage variety particularly widely used in Chinese cuisine.

In the 1980s, Asian flavors—and the wok—started to gain popularity among home cooks. Given the rising interest in Chinese, Japanese, and Thai cuisine, several Asian shops opened, offering ingredients that I had never seen before. Many of those products are now commonplace.

While writing recipes for green cookbooks, I became interested in vegetables that I hadn't used before, including bok choy. I found that it tastes great both stir-fried in a wok and finely chopped in a salad.

Fortunately, many of the Asian leaf vegetables grow elsewhere in the world. In fact, they particularly like the cool weather in northern Europe and northern America during late summer and autumn, and grow steadily and calmly. Several, including bok choy, can even tolerate a little frost. If it gets really cold, you can always move the pot into the greenhouse, where the plants will be reasonably well protected.

My first attempt to grow bok choy was not a huge success. I sowed the seeds in March and planted them out in May, but just a few weeks later, the plants shot up and started to flower. That was when I discovered that Asian vegetables are much easier to grow in cooler weather.

'Ryou' bok choy, sown in early July. The relatively late sowing means that the plants have not bolted, which can be a problem if you sow early.

KOMATSUNA

Komatsuna is another Asian leaf vegetable. It is similar to bok choy, and you can cook it in the same ways. I hadn't heard of komatsuna until I came across it in a seed catalog. It is easy to grow, which is great because I have become quite fond of it as part of my fall kitchen.

Although komatsuna is not very well known here in Denmark, it has a Danish name—spinach mustard—that describes its flavor. It can withstand a few degrees of frost, and the cold makes the taste sweeter and less sharp.

In mild winters, there is a good chance komatsuna will survive unscathed. If it does, cut the leaves a few centimeters above the root at harvest time. Then, in early spring, when it starts to get a little warmer, the plant will sprout fresh leaves, which are especially welcome at that time of year.

MIZUNA

I only recently discovered, while hunting for seeds, that mizuna, which originates from Japan, belongs to the cabbage family. For several years, I believed it to be a salad vegetable like arugula, as it has a similar but milder taste. The plant forms a rosette of finely cut, slightly feathery leaves with crisp and juicy stems.

There are several varieties, with both dark and green leaves. All of them look beautiful in a salad bowl, where they add a little more texture and body than typical salad leaves.

As with other Asian vegetables, I wait until the end of June to sow mizuna. Not so much because of the risk of early flowering, like with bok choy and komatsuna, because that's less of an issue with mizuna. However, there is another snake in paradise to contend with—flea beetles. They often attack the plants in May or June and gnaw tiny holes in the leaves.

You can buy seed mixtures with different varieties specifically intended for growing *baby leaves*. Sow them early. They may attract flea beetles, but even if they do, it's only a minor cosmetic problem.

You can eat the leaves at any stage of their development. If you let them grow over fall and winter, they will be quite big and the leaves more robust. Even so, they are still delicious when finely chopped and stir-fried in a wok.

Instead of pulling the plant out of the ground at harvest time, encourage it to sprout again by cutting or trimming the leaves just above the root.

Opposite Top: Komatsuna 'Comred' with its incredibly decorative red foliage

Opposite Bottom Left: Mizuna 'Red Devil'

Opposite Bottom Right: Mizuna 'Sheriff'

KALE

Kale is one of my favorite container crops, first and foremost, because it is so beautiful and hardy, even down to around –4°F (–20°C). This makes it a real winter vegetable. It is even said to develop a slightly sweeter, more aromatic flavor when exposed to frost. At one point, I asked one of my good friends who grows organic vegetables how much truth there is to the claim. She said that it is probably true for old varieties, but new types don't depend on the cold to taste good. That's good to know, considering how mild our winters have been lately.

When I was a child, we always had kale at New Years, and it is also part of many families' Christmas lunch in Denmark. But in recent years, I have really started to use fresh kale in the kitchen as an important winter ingredient. It is delicious finely chopped in a salad. Before mixing it with the other ingredients, I add a good oil and vinegar dressing and "massage" it into the kale so that it "absorbs" the flavors.

Opposite: 'Dwarf Green Curled' is a low-growing kale particularly suitable for pots.

Top: 'Emerald Ice' is a multicolored variety that gradually turns pale as the cold sets in.

Bottom: There are also red varieties of kale, 'Redbor' being a fairly common one.

People have been growing different types of cabbage since time immemorial, here in Denmark, all the way back to the Viking Age, when kitchen gardens were simply called cabbage gardens. According to *The Dictionary of the Danish Language*, it was a "garden with cabbage and other kitchen herbs." In the early Viking Age, the Vikings grew various types of wild cabbage. Starting in the Middle Ages, they began to grow kale, which became a staple ingredient on a par with rye bread and beer. It was said that "wherever there were good cabbage gardens, disease did not spread." Kale was mainly used in soup, called *potage*, which was made by leaving a potful of kale, and possibly onions and leeks, simmering over the fire all day. The soup was thickened with buckwheat or bread. If you could afford it, or if it was Christmas, meat and spices might also be added.

Kale is not only associated with Christmas in a culinary context. In the old days, kale stalks were used as Christmas trees, particularly an old German variety, 'Ostfriesische Palme', which can grow up to 6 feet (2 m) tall. The lower leaves mostly serve as animal feed, while the upper leaves are used in the kitchen.

Due to its high tolerance of cold and frost, kale has a very long season. If you don't get around to eating it before the following spring, it will produce beautiful light-yellow flowers.

I sow a couple of batches per season—in March and in late June. The main reason I start so early is because kale is so decorative. It looks beautiful in summer alongside all the other crops. I start harvesting the tender, aromatic leaves early on, as they are perfect for salads. I then sow for the second time to make sure I have enough kale for the winter.

Top: 'Dwarf Green Curled'
Bottom: 'Redbor'

Top: The Tuscan kale 'Nero di Toscana' in full leaf.

Opposite: The green Brussels sprouts are 'Groninger'. At the bottom left is a red variety, 'Red Bull'.

TUSCAN KALE

Tuscan kale is a special variety of kale, called palm kale here in Denmark because it resembles a palm tree, especially when it grows tall and the lower leaves have been picked. Sometimes called dinosaur kale in the United States, it is relatively new in Denmark, at least compared to regular kale, but has become an important ingredient in Nordic cuisine. In Italy, Tuscan kale has a long history, especially around Tuscany, where it has been used for generations in soups and stews.

BRUSSELS SPROUTS

Brussels sprouts are a true winter member of the cabbage family. I sow in March and enjoy the beautiful plants throughout the season. First, a strong stalk develops with long-stemmed, smooth leaves and a dense rosette at the top. In late summer, small, head-shaped buds form at the leaf junctures. When the sprouts are the size of small walnuts, they are ready to be picked by cutting them off at the point where they join the stalk.

Some people say they don't like Brussels sprouts but tend to change their mind when they try them stir-fried or thinly sliced in a salad.

HERBS

Basil, chives, dill, parsley, thyme, and rosemary are some of the more well-known herbs that are staples in my kitchen. But there are so many other exciting and flavorful herbs. As I have grown more vegetables and other edible crops in pots, I have also expanded my collection of herbs.

Fresh herbs are incredibly popular, and more and more unusual ones are popping up on the market. Very few people have heard of cola wormwood, tea flower, and oyster plant. I certainly hadn't until I became obsessed with growing herbs! I will also introduce some of the lesser-known ones in this section.

Herbs are a vast and comprehensive topic, and this section covers only a handful of species. There are plenty of good books on the subject.

Herbs can be bought in lots of different places, and the most common ones are readily available in garden centers. Look for a local supplier with a wide selection. If you can't find something locally, look for a mail order source.

DILL

Freshly cut dill on new potatoes is as indispensable as salt on eggs. It tastes of sun and summer, which is why I always sow it in generous quantities—three or four times during the spring and late summer, a few weeks apart. In my experience, it can be difficult to get the seeds to sprout in summer. Conversely, don´t sow too late, as dill can´t tolerate subzero temperatures. The first hint of frost will make it collapse.

The reason it is a good idea to sow several times is that, unlike basil and chives, dill plants don´t regrow after you cut them back. They will produce a few side shoots, but they are not very useful.

I mainly grow dill to use the green leaves, but the flowers and seeds also have their uses in the kitchen.

The Growing Process

When buying seeds, it is important to bear in mind that some varieties have been specially developed for leaf dill. These have strong foliage and don´t flower as quickly, like the varieties ´Hera´ and ´Superdukat´.

Dill does not like its roots to be disturbed, so sow the seeds well apart in the pot. Inevitably, the seedlings will be a little uneven, so thin them out to leave about 2 inches (5 cm) between each one. When the plants grow, harvest every second one so that the remaining ones have extra space. This way, you will get fairly large, well-developed plants with lots of greenery.

It is important to make sure that the plants don´t start to bolt and flower, because that will make them lose their delicate flavor. If this happens anyway, just enjoy the beautiful yellow-green umbels, which are a bonus in any bouquet. The umbels and seeds are also essential ingredients if you are pickling gherkins, cucamelons, or green beans, for example. Dill seeds also add a nice flavor to schnapps and vinegar.

Top: 'Coldasil' tolerates the cold well, grows quickly, and has a high yield. Absolutely worth looking out for.

Opposite Top: With its dark foliage, 'Dark Opal' looks particularly beautiful in a salad.

Opposite Bottom: 'Red Ball' is a relatively new, weather-resistant variety with a strong aroma.

BASIL

Basil is the herb I use most, especially in the summer.

Fresh basil is a must in a tomato salad and really brings out the flavor combination. There are around sixty species of basil, including lemon, cinnamon, and camphor. The most common is sweet basil (*Ocimum basilicum*), which has aromatic, green oval leaves and white flowers.

In warm summers, basil does well outdoors in pots and other containers, but when it gets cold and windy, I move them into the greenhouse.

Fresh basil leaves are used in a huge range of dishes, but pesto is a clear favorite. The basic recipe is simple: mix fresh basil leaves with good olive oil, Parmesan cheese, pine nuts, and garlic. Variations include using pecorino instead of Parmesan and almonds instead of pine nuts.

The Growing Process

It is relatively easy to grow basil from seed, but if you want to get a head start, buy a pot of basil at the grocery store. Although it looks bushy and dense at first glance, it actually consists of a number of individual plants. Separate the roots and plant them in individual pots with nutrient-enriched soil. Another option is to plant a dozen or so plants in a larger pot, approximately 8 inches (20 cm) in diameter. I recommend planting them fairly deep.

I let my basil plants grow in the greenhouse. Once they take root and the weather is warmer, I move them outdoors.

Basil grows quite quickly. Pluck the first leaves when the plants are about $2\frac{1}{2}$ to 3 inches (6 to 8 cm) tall. Then cut back the top shoots to about 0.2 inches (5 mm) above the second-highest pair of leaves. This encourages the plants to "bush," because new shoots will emerge from the leaf nodes. Cutting them makes them branch out again, creating a kind of snowball effect.

Propagation from Cuttings

You can also propagate basil from cuttings. The best and easiest way to do this is to let cut shoots take root in water. As I will discuss later in this chapter, I have had great success with planting rosemary cuttings in moist soil. But that method doesn't work well with basil, as the stems are not rigid enough.

To propagate basil, cut 4-inch (10 cm) shoots from a plant before it starts to flower—this is important. Remove the leaves from the lower part of the shoots, then place the shoots in water in a small, opaque container. The lack of light makes the roots grow faster. It typically takes about three weeks before the cuttings are ready for potting.

Opposite: 'African Blue' is one of the most beautiful basil varieties, not least because of its delicate purple flowers. It is relatively easy to overwinter indoors. I grow it primarily for ornamental purposes, as the leaves have a slightly sharp taste.

CHIVES

Chives are another quintessential summer kitchen herb. They add the finishing touch to an egg or potato sandwich and are indispensable in salad bowls and sprinkled over omelets and lobscouse (a hearty northern European stew).

The green shoots sprout from the ground in April and are ready to harvest when they're about 2½ inches (6 cm) tall. If you sow them, it's best to leave the plants alone for the first season.

Chives are perennials. They are also monocotyledonous, like grass, which means you can keep cutting them throughout the season and they will just keep growing.

If you're not quick off the mark with the shears, beautiful purple flowers will appear, which are also tasty and incredibly beautiful as a garnish. However, stems with flowers are not as delicate as those without, so I suggest cutting back the plants, removing the flowering stems, and serving the rest. When the plant is pruned after flowering, it simply sprouts again. If it is not pruned, the flowers will produce seeds, and the plant will slip into dormancy.

During the summer, chive plants are sometimes attacked by a kind of red, spotty fungus called chive rust. If that happens, then the only option is to cut the plant back completely and dispose of all the green parts. It is best not to harvest any more during that season. Chive rust doesn't kill the plant, so the plant will probably come back next year.

Chive rust attacks only the common chive with purple flowers, *Allium schoenoprasum*. But there is another species that does not get rust: Chinese chives (*Allium tuberosum*), also called Chinese garlic chives. It has white flowers, and the leaves have a stronger, garlic-like flavor.

Chinese chives (Allium tuberosum) produce sweet white flowers. The leaves taste like garlic.

The Growing Process

Apart from rust, growing chives is very straightforward. It's easy to sow them and get them to sprout. Sow in March, in trays with small cells—about ten seeds in each—and lightly cover the seeds. When the plants are about 2 inches (5 cm) tall, put them in individual pots with nutrient-enriched potting soil and let them grow. Later in the season, move them to larger pots. You can harvest in late summer, but as mentioned, it is better to wait until the following year.

If you don't have the patience to wait for the seeds to sprout, you can buy live chive plants at the garden center and replant them. A pot with a diameter of 6 to 8 inches (15 to 20 cm) is suitable for three plants.

When the plants are a couple of years old, it is a good idea to divide them and repot in fresh soil. This gives you more plants and revitalizes the chives. Divide the root ball, which consists of numerous small plants, into small groups of four or five. Pot them individually, and leave them to grow before transferring to containers.

When a chive plant is a couple of years old, you can divide it into multiple pieces and replant them. This gives the plant a new lease on life!

PARSLEY

There are two types of parsley: curly (*Petroselinum crispum*) and flat leaf (Petroselinum sativum). Both are a must in the kitchen and, fortunately, both thrive in pots, which means you can cut fresh greens throughout the summer. In the first year, don't harvest until mid-June, and when you do start, don't cut the plants all the way down to the ground. Cut the outer eaves only, leaving the strongest ones in the middle. It's all about photosynthesis.

The plants usually do well in the winter, especially if you keep them under cover so they don't get too wet, which can cause rot. During the winter, they don't need as much water because they are no longer growing.

The following spring, you can start harvesting once the green leaves are established, but don't wait too long. Parsley is a biennial that starts to bolt and flower in early summer of its second year. If this happens, the leaves become too tough to eat, and you'll need to start a new batch to have a supply again by midsummer.

When they hear the word parsley, most people think of the curly type, which is great for making parsley sauce. My grandma used to have a good old-fashioned parsley chopper, which was an essential item for any well-equipped kitchen back

then. They are not so common anymore, and I've never owned one. It is much easier to chop with a knife, which also means the parsley retains its distinctive texture.

When the parsley shows signs of bolting, I discard some of the plants and keep the rest, partly because I think the white umbellate flowers are beautiful and partly because I want to harvest seeds. That way, I know the seeds are fresh when I sow them.

When harvesting seeds, it is important to note that curly-leaf and flat-leaf parsley often cross-pollinate, which means that the offspring may not be identical to the plant from which you harvest the seeds.

Flat-leaf parsley has an even stronger flavor than curly parsley, and I often use whole leaves in salads, for example. Not only do they have a lovely flavor, but their dark-green color also adds beautiful depth to a bowl of baby spinach, watercress, and lamb's lettuce.

The Growing Process

It can be a little tricky to get parsley seeds to sprout. In fact, it can take six to eight weeks—and sometimes it just doesn't work. I sow in the greenhouse in early March and have had reasonably good results with seeds that I harvested the previous summer. The seeds germinate best in partial shade. Similarly, once the plants emerge, it is advisable to keep the pot out of direct sunlight.

If your attempts at growing from seed are unsuccessful, don't despair. Buy live parsley at the grocery store or garden center, separate the plants, and repot them. A 12-inch (30 cm) pot is suitable for a dozen plants.

THYME

Although most people associate thyme with the Mediterranean, there are several species that evolved elsewhere, including narrow-leaved thyme (*Thymus serpyllum*) and broad-leaved thyme (*Thymus pulegioides*). They are very similar, but as the names suggest, their foliage differs. Both are short plants with creeping stems and small green leaves that give off an aromatic smell if you rub them between your fingers.

There are around fifty species of Mediterranean thyme, including common thyme (*Thymus vulgaris*), also known as garden thyme or medicinal thyme.

The mild winters of recent years have made it possible for me to grow southern European species in pots, because I can just move them indoors when the weather is too cold. Having said that, too much moisture is a bigger problem than the cold. It's important that you plant your thyme—whether in pots or beds—in soil mixed with gravel and/or small stones so that the water can drain away (more on this later).

Historically, Denmark doesn't have much of a tradition of fresh herbs in our food, at least not compared to some other countries, but thyme is the exception that proves the rule. Cookbooks from the eighteenth century often mention thyme, especially in recipes for sausages. In fact, the Danes even used to call thyme the "sausage herb."

Thyme was also used in slaughterhouses, where intestines would be placed in water along with thyme to remove the unpleasant odor. Slaughtering usually took place in November, a time of year when fresh thyme was rarely available, especially given the harsh winters back then, so thyme was harvested in the fall and hung up to dry for use in winter.

Wealthy farmers even let their pigs eat thyme, believing it made the meat taste more like wild boar. Thyme was also used in home remedies for sore throats and colds because it helps to clear mucus.

I cook with thyme a lot in the fall and winter and sprinkle it liberally into stews and oven dishes. When seasoning with thyme, beware—the flavor grows stronger the longer the dish cooks. Thyme is also included in blends like herbes de Provence and *bouquet garni*. The latter is a bundle of herbs tied together with string. A classic bouquet garni consists of parsley, thyme, and bay leaves. You can also use thyme to make drinks like spiced schnapps and herbal tea.

I grow several different types of thyme, which vary not only in their flavor but also in their flowers, which can be white, violet, or purple, depending on the species. When the tiny flowers bloom in late summer, they form a beautiful, highly eye-catching display that bees seem to love.

The flowers are also edible and look beautiful when lightly sprinkled over a dish.

One type of thyme of which I am particularly fond is lemon thyme, which has distinctive, yellow-speckled leaves. The delicate taste of lemon adds an extra little kick to the characteristic thyme flavor.

The Growing Process

Plant your thyme in well-drained soil. I use seed-starting soil that has a low nutrient content, mixed with sharp gravel and small stones. To keep the plants healthy and dense, cut them back by about half each spring and immediately after flowering.

ROSEMARY

Some ingredients seem inextricably linked. Just think of basil and mozzarella. The same is true of rosemary and lamb. They're quite simply made for each other. When the aroma of oven-roasted lamb with rosemary and garlic spreads through the kitchen, it's pure bliss.

Rosemary is also a must for focaccia, herb butter, and herb vinegar.

If you have been to the Mediterranean, you can't have failed to notice the many wild rosemary bushes, which grow to an impressive size. In some parts of France, rosemary is even used as fuel. It must give off a wonderful aroma!

Old herb books claim that rosemary, as well as its culinary value, has a wide range of other properties:

- Sniffing a sprig of rosemary keeps you young forever
- Burning rosemary disinfects the air
- Rosemary sprigs in drawers and cupboards keep moths away
- Shampoo with rosemary stimulates the roots and gives your hair strength and shine
- Ointments containing rosemary are used to treat muscle pain and have a positive effect on circulation
- Rosemary aids digestion and relieves fatigue and headaches.

If the summer is warm and the weather good, rosemary produces the most beautiful, lavender-blue flowers, which are just as edible as the aromatic leaves. This variety grows almost horizontally and is known as creeping rosemary.

Cuttings

Rosemary seems to have been quite hardy during the mild winters of recent years—certainly in my garden. But to be on the safe side, I take cuttings in the early summer. It's not difficult: Cut 4- to 5-inch (10 to 12 cm)-long top shoots from the plant. Remove the needles from the lower part of each shoot, and then stick them in a pot filled with moist seed-starting mix. To help roots form, place the shoots close to the edge of the pot and keep the surrounding area moist. As shown in the photograph, the best way to do this is by using a plastic bag with a hole in it to provide ventilation.

The shoots will take root after a month or so. Once the roots start to poke through the holes in the bottom of the pot, it is time to repot them into individual pots, but make sure the pots are not too large. After that, repot them gradually as they grow.

It is fairly easy to propagate rosemary from cuttings, especially if you cover them with a plastic bag. Remember to cut a ventilation hole though. Too much moisture can rot the cuttings.

SAGE

There are an incredible number of sage species, some of which are good for cooking. As they originate from the Mediterranean region, they all have one thing in common—they love the sun. They also produce beautiful flowers, and some have healing properties.

One of the best-known plants used for medicinal purposes is medicinal sage, *Salvia officinalis*, which was brought north by monks in the Middle Ages. We have known for thousands of years that plants can cure diseases, injuries, and ailments. Records of medicinal plants were made in China as early as 3000 BCE, and in ancient Egyptian papyrus scrolls from 1600 BCE onwards. About a thousand years later, the Greek physician Hippocrates (circa 460 BCE to approximately 370 BCE), known as the father of Western medicine, used various plants and herbs for medicinal purposes. He described many of them in his highly influential work *Corpus Hippocraticum*.

In the Middle Ages, the first monasteries were founded in Denmark, and medicinal plants were cultivated in the gardens. Monks and nuns were key figures in the treatment of disease throughout Europe. The German abbess Hildegard of Bingen (circa 1098–1179) is particularly worthy of mention. Known as Saint Hildegard, she greatly expanded knowledge of herbal remedies and has been called the most important woman of the Middle Ages.

The oldest Danish herbal medicine book is the handwritten *Liber herbarum* (*Book of Herbs*) by Henrik Harpestreng (died 1244). Not much is known about Harpestreng other than that he was a royal physician and canon of Roskilde Cathedral. *Liber herbarum* became widely known throughout most of the Nordic region and remained in use right up to the twentieth century.

It is not known for certain where Harpestreng grew his herbs, but the garden called after him at the open-air Viking museum in Lejre re-creates how it may have looked and includes many of the plants he used, including medicinal sage.

Medicinal sage is often uniformly green, but there are also a few beautiful varieties with multicolored foliage. These include 'Berggarten Variegated', seen on the left. The variety on the right is called 'Tricolor'.

Professional gardener Camilla Plum has this to say about sage:

It's good for sore throats, blocked noses, restlessness, nervousness, sore stomachs, and poor digestion. Sage tea, made from fresh leaves with honey and lemon, tastes great, too.

And medicinal sage is simply one of the most amazing and tastiest herbs ever. It is grown and cared for in exactly the same way as lavender, and the two also look very, very beautiful together in the kitchen garden and in the perennial bed.

Medicinal sage is a very variable plant: it comes with long, narrow leaves and with almost completely round ones. It comes in varied shades of green, some almost gray. They can be smooth or fuzzy, but they are all wrinkled. There are a multitude of colorful varieties—red-leaved, yellow-veined, even one with red, green, and white leaves. In my experience, they all taste exactly the same—and good.

The round-leaved variety is incredibly lush, but flowers very sparsely. The colorful varieties are a little more delicate—and also slow to flower. But they usually cope well with winter.

However, the ordinary variety, which you can buy in pots at the supermarket, blooms so lavishly and beautifully that it takes your breath away.

If you really want to try eating sage, you should grow the largest-leaved variety you can find. These leaves can be used to make an incredibly refined snack or tapas by simply dipping them in batter, frying them in olive oil until crispy, and eating them warm, sprinkled with flaky sea salt. They taste absolutely wonderful.

You can also fry sage leaves quickly in oil until they are crispy, then sprinkle them over salads or a piece of fried fish or veal.

Overall, sage is excellent with veal and pork. Fry the sage leaves in the pan with the meat and use plenty—a handful is enough for four people. Sage is almost essential for veal liver. Fry the leaves with the liver and deglaze the pan with vermouth, lemon juice, and add a knob of butter towards the end.

There are many fragrant types of sage with descriptive names, including black currant, apple, and honeydew melon. The latter smells almost like popsicles if you run your hand over the leaves and then put your fingers to your nose. It adds a subtle flavor to a jug of ice water and can also be used to make tea.

'Honey Melon' is an exquisite sage for tea and juice. It also produces beautiful fiery-red flowers that brighten up cakes and desserts.

FRENCH TARRAGON

There are two types of tarragon, Russian and French, and I would recommend the latter, which has a stronger flavor and is much more aromatic. Unfortunately, the Russian version is often sold instead. You can propagate the Russian variety from seed, but you have to propagate French tarragon from cuttings, which is more difficult.

French tarragon, which grows to a height of 28 to 32 inches (70 to 80 cm), has narrow, lanceolate, dark-green leaves with a delicate anise flavor. Tarragon is best known as an ingredient in béarnaise sauce, but it is also delicious in soups, salads, vinegar, and herb butter. French chefs often refer to tarragon as the queen of herbs.

The distinctive anise flavor is not to everyone's taste, but I can't get enough of fennel, tarragon, and Thai basil. It is also worth mentioning *Tagetes lucida*, known as Mexican mint marigold or Texas tarragon, the leaves and taste of which are similar to tarragon. This is a short plant with small yellow flowers, which is propagated from seed. It will behave like a perennial if it is overwintered in a frost-free environment.

Spiced Schnapps

Spiced schnapps is a wonderful way to preserve and enjoy delicate flavors. If you love the flavor of licorice, I highly recommend making anise schnapps, which is a great accompaniment to herring or other fish.

You will need a bottle of flavorless schnapps or vodka (24 fluid ounces, or 710 ml), 5 to 6 tarragon sprigs, half a fennel bulb, 4 to 5 teaspoons of fennel seeds, and 2 to 3 prunes.

Dice the fennel bulb and roast the seeds. Place them in a bottle along with the tarragon and prunes. Pour in the schnapps or vodka. Let the schnapps steep for a week, shaking it daily. Then filter it into a carafe or bottle, and let it rest for a couple of weeks.

The prunes not only sweeten the schnapps but also endow it with a beautiful, deep color. You can also use honey as a sweetener or leave out the sweetness altogether. The great thing about spiced schnapps is that you can adjust it to your preference. If you think it tastes too mild, let it steep a little longer. If the taste is too strong, you can dilute it with more schnapps or vodka.

When it comes to different flavor combinations for schnapps, the possibilities are endless. There are lots of different recipes available online using herbs and berries.

MINT

There is one particularly good reason to grow mint in containers. It spreads like a weed and can soon become a nuisance. After all, even if you love mojitos, mint jelly, and mint tea, there are limits to how much mint you need. If the plant starts to look a little tired in the summer, simply cut it back to the base and new, fresh foliage will quickly sprout. When the mint starts to fill the pot after a season or two, dig it up, divide it into smaller pieces, and plant it again. You will soon have plenty of mint.

Mint comes in many different species, but apart from the uses mentioned above, there is not a great tradition of using it in Danish cuisine. In other cultures, mint is as ubiquitous as parsley. In Morocco, for example, mint is as much a part of the culinary DNA as cumin, turmeric, saffron, basil, cinnamon, ginger, and apricots.

Few herbs have such a varied range of scents as mint. Apple, pineapple, and kiwi are just a few examples, but the best-known mint is undoubtedly peppermint (*Mentha piperita*). It is grown for its rich content of volatile oils, including menthol, and is used to make toothpaste, liqueurs, candy, and essential oils, among other products.

My favorite mint for making jelly is apple mint (*Mentha suaveolens*), which is identifiable not only by its apple-like scent but by its light, soft, and fuzzy leaves. It is delicious chopped in salads.

As mentioned earlier, lamb is often associated with rosemary, but we should also mention mint in this context too. In Britain in particular, mint is a must with lamb, whether it's apple-mint jelly or mint sauce, which is made from chopped mint leaves, white wine vinegar, sugar, and boiling water. Simple but incredibly tasty.

Spearmint (*Mentha spicata*) is another popular species, largely because it is used in mojitos. Just as mojitos are synonymous with mint, the popular Cuban drink is synonymous with Ernest Hemingway. There is even a special Hemingway mint variety, 'Nemorosa', which connoisseurs consider the best kind for the classic cocktail. It is said to originate from the backyard of the bar in Havana where the famous author enjoyed his mojitos. The Hemingway mint is available from several retailers.

Here is an easy and simple mojito recipe for one person: 6 to 8 large mint leaves, half an organic lime, 1 tablespoon cane sugar, 1.7 fluid ounces (50 ml) rum, 3.4 fluid ounces (100 ml) sparkling water, and 3.4 fluid ounces (100 ml) crushed ice. You will also need a muddler, a bartending tool used to mash and crush fruit and spices.

Put the mint leaves, lime, and sugar in a glass, and mash them together. Pour the rum, sparkling water, and ice into the glass, and garnish with a few mint leaves before serving.

The multiple potential variations include replacing some of the sparkling water with juice—I often use rhubarb—and it also tastes great with berries. Use around six to eight berries per glass, and muddle them together with the other ingredients. You can also, of course, make a nonalcoholic version by omitting the rum.

Opposite Top: Like all other varieties of mint, apple mint has lovely, delicate flowers.

Opposite Bottom: Strawberry mint grows upright and has small leaves with a hint of strawberry scent.

Bottom: Spearmint for mojitos

LEMON BALM

Lemon balm is easy to grow in containers. Like mint, it is perennial, hardy, and lush. Keep harvesting, and the plant will sprout again and again. At the end of the season, I let it bloom, as the flowers are very pretty in bouquets. Later, you can harvest the seeds, which are very easy to germinate—as is evident in my garden from the numerous shoots that pop up between the paving in spring.

The delicate leaves make a beautiful garnish on cakes and desserts, along with berries. Use lemon balm whenever you need a citrus flavor. Finely chopped leaves add a delicious flavor to fish and are also a refined addition to salads. It also works well in spiced vinegar and schnapps.

Lemon balm makes a wonderful tea: Just put a handful of fresh leaves in a teapot, pour boiling water over them, and cover with a lid. The lid prevents the essential oils from evaporating. Steep for five minutes, strain the leaves, and serve.

Lemon balm has small, fuzzy leaves that are a great addition to any dessert or cake, especially alongside berries.

OREGANO

Oregano or marjoram? Two sides of the same coin, perhaps, but there are slight differences. The botanical name for oregano is *Origanum vulgare*, but there is also a species called *Origanum majorana*. I find it difficult to taste the difference between the two. I grow *Origanum vulgare* in my garden. Connoisseurs say its slightly sweet and spicy flavor is the more refined of the two.

As mentioned earlier, some herbs are closely associated with specific ingredients and dishes. This is also true of oregano, which is an important part of Italian cuisine, especially pizza. It is also good in tomato sauce. In winter, I often use it in soups, stews, and oven dishes. Don't use too much, though, as the flavor can become overpowering. To prevent this, make a bouquet garni by tying together a few stems with leaves, and remove it from the dish when you think the flavor is just right.

Oregano is fairly hardy and also grows wild here in Denmark in sandy soils. In containers, it grows a bit like thyme, and it is a good idea to prune in the spring and after flowering.

This variety is called 'Hot and Spicy' because of its extra-strong flavor.

BAY LEAVES

Bay leaves are another kitchen staple, both fresh and dried. They taste best when green, but the dried leaves retain their flavor for a long time, especially when stored in a dry, cool place.

I really like the perfumed flavor of bay leaves. When I roast pork or ribs, I stick halved leaves between every third or fourth layer of fat. Both the flavor and the aroma are absolutely enchanting. If you use bay leaves in a roast dish, I recommend adding leaves at the beginning and cooking them along with onions, for example, because roasting releases the essential oils.

When I boil meat or fish, I often add a green bay leaf. The same applies to rice, beans, and lentils. And bay leaves are absolutely essential when pickling beets.

As bay, also known as bay laurel, originates from southern climes, it is a good idea to grow it in pots in northern latitudes. It can cope with temperatures a few degrees below zero, but bring it indoors when the weather is cold.

Bay laurel trees are grown for their culinary value and because the shrub/tree is ideal for topiary. For hundreds of years, people have been cutting evergreen plants into different shapes. As early as the 1400s, it was the fashion in Italian and French Renaissance gardens to divide up the grounds using straight, precisely trimmed boxwood hedges. By the end of the 1600s, the style changed to Baroque, but topiary remained popular. The Baroque garden was similarly strict and symmetrical, with axial avenues, fountains, and parterre beds, surrounded by laurel topiary and cone-shaped shrubs.

LOVAGE

Lovage (*Levisticum officinale*) has a complex, nuanced flavor profile. It is a classic ingredient, especially when boiling potatoes, but you have to be careful not to use too much. A single, thin stalk with leaves is enough. I also use lovage when baking meatballs or frying traditional Danish *frikadeller*—I place a few leaves in the pan with melted butter before adding the meat.

It's as if lovage has been almost forgotten. I learned about it from my grandma, who had it in her herb garden. When the scent wafts through my kitchen, it brings back many fond memories.

Lovage is a perennial that originated in the Mediterranean. Like many other herbs, it was introduced to Scandinavia by monks who used it for medicinal purposes. In this context, the species name *officinale*, derived from the Latin term for an apothecary's workshop, makes perfect sense.

In garden beds, lovage grows fairly large, reaching a height of around 6½ feet (2 m). It doesn't grow that big in a container, but that's not a problem—as mentioned, you don't need much to season a dish.

Earlier, I talked about pesto made from basil, but you can use other types of greens, such as parsley, kale, and lovage. Lovage pesto makes a great dressing for potato salad and also tastes delicious on toast. All types of pesto are, of course, perfect when stirred through warm pasta.

SAVORY

Savory is an ancient herb but is not very well known, which is surprising. It is quite easy to grow and very tasty. It was used more in the past and deserves a renaissance. Savory was really popular in ancient Rome. It tastes quite similar to pepper, which was difficult to obtain at the time.

Monks took the plant with them throughout Europe and planted it in monastery gardens, from where it spread and acquired several nicknames, including poor man's spice, pepper herb, and bean herb—the latter because it adds an excellent flavor to bean dishes.

The flavor is quite delicate, but you have to be careful not to use too much, because it can easily overpower. I sometimes use it in meat dishes, such as on the rare occasions that I make a meat roll with lamb. When finely chopped, it is a good addition to salad. As well as tasting like pepper, it also has notes of thyme and oregano, which makes it a multifaceted herb. Savory has more than earned its place in the well-known French blend herbes de Provence.

There are two types of savory—winter (*Satureja montana*) and summer (*Satureja hortensis*). The latter is an annual plant sown from seed in early spring. It grows up to 16 inches (40 cm) tall, with thin, branched stems. As an aside, in ancient times, monks were forbidden to eat summer savory, as it was used as an aphrodisiac!

Once the frost sets in, summer savory season is over, and it is winter savory's turn to shine. This is a somewhat different plant, a hardy evergreen dwarf shrub resistant to the winter chill. It is a perennial and looks beautiful all year round.

As mentioned, there are both summer and winter varieties of savory. Both of those shown are winter savory, but the one in front is a creeping variety. Winter savory has small, white flowers that bloom in the summer.

WOOD SORREL

Wood sorrel and white sorrel are two different names for the same plant. *Oxalis corniculata*. In a culinary context, it is referred to most often as wood sorrel due to its sour taste. There is another type of sorrel, *Oxalis acetosella*, a wild green species that grows all over Europe, especially on the forest floor in spring.

Wood sorrel has dark or bronze leaves that look extremely pretty as the long stems cascade over the edge of their pots. In fact, this plant is so beautiful that you may be tempted to plant it in a bed—don't! It will become an extremely troublesome weed that is virtually impossible to get rid of. I speak from experience. A few years ago, I bought a couple of dark-leaved wood sorrel and planted them in my beds. It was everywhere within a couple of seasons.

As a light sprinkling on a salad, both the leaves and flowers are beautiful. They have a tart flavor that adds a little zing. The sour taste comes from oxalic acid, which is also found in rhubarb.

Three different varieties of wood sorrel. At the back and on the opposite page is the most common dark-leaved variety. At the front is a bronze-colored type. On the right is green wood sorrel, which grows wild in Denmark.

WATER PEPPER

I grow water pepper (*Persicaria hydropiper*) 'Rubra' primarily because of its beautiful dark leaves. You can use it in the kitchen, but be careful—this is one of the strongest herbs around. If you try to chew a leaf, you will experience a strong, warm, and tingling sensation that lasts for a while. Even a small leaf will leave a strong aftertaste for a couple of hours. It is mainly used in Asian cuisine, including sushi, salads, and soups.

It is related to knotweed and susceptible to the winter cold, so I move it indoors in the fall.

VIETNAMESE CORIANDER

Few herbs divide opinion like cilantro/coriander. Some love it and can't get enough, while others say it tastes like soap. Traditional cilantro is a bit like broad-leaved parsley—indeed, some people even call it Chinese parsley. I prefer to grow Vietnamese coriander, *Polygonum odoratum*, rather than the common variety, as it is easier. What's more, the plant will come back year after year if you protect it from frost.

It is interesting that the plant tastes like cilantro, because it is actually a knotweed, completely unrelated to common cilantro (*Coriandrum sativum*).

SORREL

Despite the similar names, sorrel and the previously mentioned wood sorrel are very different species. I mainly grow red-veined sorrel (*Rumex sanguineus*) for the beautiful leaves, which I use when very tender, usually in salads. Once they are bigger, they are no use in the kitchen, so pick them before they grow too much.

As the plant grows, it begins to resemble wild green sorrel. The flowers are nothing to write home about, and you should definitely cut them off before they shed seeds, as the self-sowing plants become rampant.

Opposite Top: Water pepper
Opposite Bottom Left: Vietnamese coriander
Opposite Bottom Right: Sorrel

CURRY PLANT

Curry plant (*Helichrysum italicum*) is another gray-leaved herb. The name stems from the distinct curry scent and taste, but it is not used to make curries (which are actually made from a blend of numerous other herbs and spices, depending on the targeted flavor profile). If you know a little about plant Latin, you will know that the genus *Helichrysum* includes a long list of species you can dry and use as everlasting flowers. Fashionable in the 1970s, they are now enjoying a second lease on life, much to my surprise. One of the most popular is *Helichrysum bracteatum*, which in Danish is simply called *evighedsblomst* (everlasting flower). In English, it is known as strawflower.

Curry plants produce small, yellow flowers that you can also dry and store, but that's not why I grow them. In fact, I find the flowers a little distracting—the beautiful, needle-like leaves are decorative enough by themselves.

On a warm, breezy summer day, you can't help but notice the curry scent when you pass the plant. You might almost think that someone was making Indian food.

Like with bay leaves, you cook with curry plant stems but remove them before serving. They are great in stews, soups, and pickles.

TEA FLOWER

As the name suggests, you can make excellent tea from the tea flower (*Micromeria fruticosa*), which is also known as white-leaved savory. It is very aromatic and comes in a variety of flavors, such as menthol, citrus, and camphor. Boiling water poured over a few stems in a teapot is tasty and healthy. It has a number of medicinal properties, including being antiseptic, that inhibits or kills bacteria. You can also chop the plant finely for use in salads. But be careful not to use too much.

I grow tea flowers not only for their aroma but also because their grayish foliage is incredibly beautiful, especially when the small, white flowers bloom. They grow in mountainous areas and along the Mediterranean coast, which means they are extremely drought tolerant.

OYSTER PLANT

I find it fascinating when plants have an immediately recognizable but unexpected flavor. This is the case with the oyster plant or oyster leaf (*Mertensia maritima*), which tastes just like oysters. You would never think it looking at the grayish, fleshy leaves. The plant produces beautiful blue flowers, which are also edible.

As mentioned, the Latin name often tells us something interesting about a plant species. For example, *officinalis* indicates a medicinal plant. Here, the species name is *maritima*, which tells us that the oyster plant grows by the sea and should be planted in well-drained, sandy soil.

Serve the oyster plant raw, as the flavor disappears when cooked. It is great in fish and seafood dishes or in a salad.

LEMON VERBENA

Lemon verbena (*Aloysia citrodora*) is another plant with a citrus flavor that makes really good tea. It also goes well with fish and chicken. I finely chop the leaves and use them in marinades, salads, and occasionally in desserts.

It is a fairly heat-loving plant and doesn't like wind, so you need to keep it sheltered. It is also quite sensitive to the cold, so move it indoors or cover it in the winter. Lemon verbena sheds its leaves in winter, but that doesn't mean it's dead. You can always check if a plant is alive by scratching the bark a little. If it's green inside, it's still alive.

In spring, cut back the plant to 4 to 6 inches (10 to 15 cm), after which small leaves will slowly begin to sprout from the dormant buds. It takes a while, so be patient.

Verbena is also known as holy wort, but you rarely hear that term these days. Instead, the Latin name is usually used. A lot of gardeners know various species of verbena, like the giant ornamental version *Verbena bonariensis*, which isn't used in the kitchen.

COLA PLANT

It may sound unlikely that a plant can smell like cola, but it's true! Children in particular find this plant fascinating. The cola plant (*Artemisia abrotanum*) is delicate and decorative but quite hardy, with foliage resembling dill. It also produces small yellow or white flowers, though I have yet to see them myself! I usually cut it back to about 2 inches (5 cm) above the ground in the spring, after which it sprouts again with fresh foliage.

Although it is of little use for cooking, you can use the cola plant to make schnapps.

The cola plant is one of the many wormwood species, all of which are quite bitter and astringent. This makes them good for schnapps. Sea wormwood (*Artemisia maritima*) is particularly highly prized by schnapps enthusiasts.

Many wormwoods have decorative gray to silvery foliage, which makes them good ornamental plants. For example, wormwood is heavily featured in the White Garden at Sissinghurst Castle Garden in the south of England.

GLASSWORT

You may well have encountered fresh green shoots of glasswort (*Salicornia europaea*), also known as samphire, pickle weed, or sea asparagus, being sold at markets if you live in or visit coastal areas. It grows in salt marshes and coastal areas that flood regularly. In Denmark, it is particularly abundant in the Wadden Sea area. In the United States, glasswort can be found along both the Atlantic and Pacific coasts, as well as in salt marshes and flats around bays and the Great Lakes. There are also several North American species of glasswort that are also edible.

The crisp, tender, and juicy herb has a salty flavor. It can be used raw in salads and lightly steamed or sautéed in butter. Don't cook it for too long, as it will lose its crispness and flavor.

ABOUT THE AUTHOR

Claus Dalby has been called "the Scandinavian Martha Stewart." He is a designer, florist, and Danish gardener who has amassed a huge fan base in Scandinavia, the US, and around the world. He is also a successful publisher, television personality, and designer of glass vases for Holmegaard. His books in English include *Containers in the Garden* and *The Cottage Garden*. Claus's signature style of gardening uses densely packed plants and changing seasonal displays, often in monochromatic color palettes. He also runs an online garden club with monthly subscribers from around the world.

INDEX

THE CONTAINER KITCHEN GARDEN